THE SEVEN LAWS OF THE

SONS OF NOAH,

And how they influenced *Acts of the Apostles*

by James A. Nollet

ACKNOWLEDGEMENTS

- I would like to acknowledge and gratefully thank Matthias Rötthig of Görlitz, Germany, and Tony Roberts, Bristol, UK, for their assistance in helping me prepare working PDF's of this book.

- I also thank John Thompson of New Mexico for his assistance in so many ways – with illustrations, ISBN's, Library of Congress certifications, and general self-publishing assistance.

- And perhaps most of all, I must acknowledge and thank R. W. Peake for his kind permission and approval in borrowing two illustrations of "(Cornelius) the Good Centurion." He is the author and copyright holder of the very successful *Marching With Caesar* series. Most of the books in this dozen-volume (and growing) series are 1st-person novelized biographies of the Centurion Titus Pullus, a real-life centurion mentioned by name by Julius Caesar in his *Commentaries* of the Gallic wars. The illustrations of Pullus were created by Peake's artist Marina Shipova. The Pullus character was brought to life in the recent HBO television series *Rome*. More information about Peake and his works may be found on www.marchingwithcaesarbookseries.com.

Contents

1) INTRODUCTION 8

2) THE OLD COVENANT(S) AND THE NEW
   COVENANT 25

3) WHAT ARE THE SEVEN LAWS OF THE SONS
   OF NOAH?..30

4) THE FIRST LAW – JUSTICE 33

5) THE 7th AND LAST OF THE SEVEN LAWS OF
   THE SONS OF NOAH..49

6) THE GOOD CENTURION..57

7) CORNELIUS THE GOOD CENTURION...................65

8) CONVERTS ON THE FIRST PENTECOST – BUT
   FROM WHAT RELIGION TO WHAT RELIGION?...75

9) PAUL PREACHES IN SYNAGOGUES TO JEWS
   AND GENTILES..84

10) THE CONTRADICTION – HAS ANYONE
    SPOTTED IT? 100

11) SOMETHING REMARKABLE 104

12) THE FIRST TRIAL (HEARING) OF THE
    APOSTLE PAUL 106

13) PAUL HAD LONG ABANDONED HIS
    BELIEF IN MOSAIC LAW....................................120

14) THE SECOND TRIAL OF THE APOSTLE
    PAUL 125

15) EPILOGUE 1, THE DESPOSYNI 148

16) EPILOGUE 2: WHAT COULD HAVE BEEN? 151

The purpose of this book is to promulgate the Good News and doctrine of the Seven Laws of the Sons of Noah to the non-Jewish world, and in particular to the realm of Christendom, for a general knowledge of these Laws can save and transform our entire world.

To the Christian World, I make this promise at the outset: You should know about these Seven Laws (and will be rewarded for the effort that will be required to learn about them), for they had a profound effect on the founders of your religion, and you cannot know your own religion (or general history) properly without understanding the Seven Laws and how they affected the direction of the early Christian Church.

This book is primarily intended more for Christian readers than Jewish. While this book does contain numerous Talmudical and Biblical references which would be entirely satisfactory from a Jewish perspective, it also contains even more numerous citations from the Christian scriptures which many Jews would not be comfortable with. For this reason, and because Jews already acknowledge the truth and existence of the Seven Laws of the Sons of Noah, Jews therefore hardly need this primer on the Seven Laws to educate and encourage *their* belief.

This book therefore is primarily intended for Christian readers.

What *are* the Seven Laws of the Sons of Noah? Few Christians have ever even heard of them – and, moreover think that they are doing just fine with their Bible just as it is. Why then should Christians know or care about this first of all Covenants, one which pre-dates even the Abrahamic Covenant (Genesis 12 – 15) and the Covenant of Moses?

There are two reasons. One, according to Judaism, this Covenant binds both Jews and Christians whether Christians know it or not, and whether they like it or not, or whether they agree with it or not. For in Judaism, the Seven Laws of the Sons of Noah, taken together, *is the very first Covenant of **all** Covenants.* The "Mother of all Covenants," to paraphrase the late Saddam Hussein. It is binding upon all of mankind, Jews and non-Jews alike, and therefore incumbent upon all Christians to know.

In addition to this, Christians also need to know about this Covenant because it is impossible for a Christian to understand certain Christian scriptures correctly, most particularly Acts of the Apostles, unless and until he knows and understands what The Seven Laws of the Sons of Noah are. And Christians will readily admit that they have an affirmative obligation to understand their scriptures as well as they can.

Most of all, Christians need to know that this Covenant, agreed upon between God and Noah and his sons after the Great Flood, is one which the founders of their own Christian religion understood *and lived by*. Yes; the men who literally walked with Jesus and ran his Nazarene Church after Jesus left this world, knew of these laws and *practiced* them.

What was good enough for them therefore should be good enough for all Christians.

This book will define what these Seven Laws are and will show how the existence of the Seven Laws influenced the course of certain passages in the Gospels and Acts of the Apostles. But first the following Introduction:

1) INTRODUCTION

There is a universal belief that the Ten Commandments, given at Mt. Sinai to Moses and the Children of Israel, are universally binding upon all of mankind. Certainly, Christians feel bound by them.

However, in Judaism it is not the familiar Ten Commandments which bind all of mankind, but rather a little-known, older version, which are called *The Seven Laws of the Sons of Noah.* It may surprise and even shock Christians to learn that, according to Judaism, all non-Jews, including Christians, have *no* affirmative obligation at all to follow the 10 Commandments, or indeed any of God's Laws which proceed from the Old Testament – save for the Seven Laws.

Why does Judaism hold that the Ten Commandments are not binding upon all of mankind, but Seven Laws of the Sons of Noah are? It's because, within the context of Book of Exodus, God gave the Ten Commandments, and the entire *Torah* (Mosaic Law), only to the persons who were present at Mt. Sinai, and to their descendants. That excludes most of mankind.

Here is how the 10 Commandments commence:

I am the LORD thy God Who brought ***thee*** (which is to say, only the Children of Egypt, not the entire human race, for they are the people whom God is addressing) *out of the land of Egypt, out of the house of bondage. Thou shalt have no other gods before Me...*

(Exodus 20:2-3, translation from the Hebrew-English version published by the S. S. & R. Publishing Company of Brooklyn, NY. All Pentateuch citations are taken from this version, not the KJV.)

Since most of mankind doesn't descend from those who were at Mt. Sinai, therefore the Ten Commandments are not binding upon their descendants – at least in the opinion of Judaism. And we see, for example, most Christians do not observe the 7th day of the week as their Sabbath, and, according to Judaism, *have no obligation to do so.*

But in like manner, just as God gave the 10 Commandments to the Children of Israel and their descendants, so did God also give the Seven Laws to Noah and his sons and all their descendants. And since, by definition, Noah and his sons are the progenitors of all of mankind, it therefore follows that any divine laws which bound them and their descendants bind all of mankind to this very day, Jews as well as Christians and others.

All mankind therefore needs to learn about these laws, and how to live by them.

But a non-Jew might very well say, or ask, "Why? Why should I worry about these Seven Laws? I never even heard of them; how important could they be? And since my Bible consists of both the Old and New Testaments, the Ten Commandments do bind me, especially since I revere the Old Testament as the Word of God. And since the concept of the Seven Laws is a Jewish teaching and since I'm not a Jew, why need I pay attention to what Judaism, or rabbis, tell me? After all, I believe that my religion (Christianity) is *the* True Religion, and that it superseded and replaced Judaism, which is now a defunct religion."

And the answer is, *because the Early Church, this "better religion," established by Jesus Christ and his disciples who knew him and who walked the earth with him and listened to his words, knew of these Seven Laws of the Sons of Noah, and observed them and lived by them.* And if it were good enough for Christianity's founders, it should be good enough for their followers, the Christians of today.

The evidence for this perhaps startling claim can be found in the Christian scriptures themselves, if one but knows how to find it, and has the wit and competence to recognize what he's seeing when he sees it.

It has always been a traditional goal of pious Christians to live their lives within a church that is as much like the original, authentic church of Jesus Christ himself as is possible – "to stand under the cross with Jesus personally," so to speak. This was one reason why Dr. Martin Luther led the Reformation, since, in his belief, the Catholic Church of the time had drifted far away from the authentic Church of Jesus, and so he attempted to bring the "authentic" church, which he himself established in Germany, back to its "original" roots.

The claim here, then, is that the early Church followed and observed the Seven Laws of the Sons of Noah, and therefore, any Christian who seeks the source roots of his religion should learn about the Seven Laws. But where then does a *Christian* find this evidence?

Much of this may be found in Acts of the Apostles. Admittedly, without a knowledge of what the Seven Laws are, it will be difficult for a Christian to recognize such passages, but after he or she learns about the Seven Laws, certain passages in Acts actually jump off the page and become crystal-clear. Indeed, it may fairly be said that it is impossible to understand Acts of the Apostles correctly without an understanding of the Seven Laws of the Sons of Noah. And therefore, this provides yet another reason to learn about the Seven Laws, since Christians should always strive to understand their own scriptures better.

But where can anybody find Biblical, or Old Testament, evidence for the existence of the Seven Laws of the Sons of Noah?

Some time ago, I have a conversation with a Chassidic rabbi in Brooklyn, New York, USA, and he urged me to tell all the non-Jews I could find about the Seven Laws of the Sons of Noah. Scholem Ber told me (in his humble opinion), it is my job, and is why God placed me on earth, and perhaps in particular in the heart of Europe at this time. (I now live in Lower Silesia, SW Poland.)

And I answered, but how can I show this to them? They will expect me to prove my claim. And he replied, just tell them that it's in the "Holy Torah." And I answered, but they don't understand "Holy Torah" as you do. (Rabbi Scholem Ber of course believes that "Holy Torah" is not only the written Bible, but is also the vast universe of Talmud and other commentaries.)

* * *

Here I want to interject something. I now write the following words several months after I finished the rest of this manuscript, and had already sent a draft version of it to my former publisher. A certain pastor (the publisher's husband) reviewed it, and he wrote back to me saying that my arguments were "more Talmudical than Biblical." The pastor did *not* mean that as a compliment; he meant it as a *criticism*. Why? Because this pastor is a working Protestant minister with his own congregation and, to him, the Word of God is *sola scriptura*. That is to say, only the *written* Bible is the Word of God – naturally which he defines as the written Old and New Testaments. *All* other things which claim to be the Word of God, therefore, are *not* the Word of God. That includes the Koran of Islam, *but it also includes the Talmud.*

And you don't believe that a pastor, or Christians in general, could feel this way? Then consider the words taken from the Statement of Belief of a certain Christian radio station somewhere in North America on the subject

"*Sola Scriptura*" (which means in Latin, "only [written] scripture")

"Waves of Power (that is what this station calls itself) accepts the Hebrew (that is to say, the Old Testament) and Greek (that is to say, the New Testament) Scriptures as the only authority by which everything is judged. There is no room for human tradition or opinions of clergy."

Many, many Christian churches and media outlets (admittedly, mostly Protestant / Evangelical, not Catholic so much) expressly say the same thing in their respective Statements of Belief.

To this pastor, any claim that the Talmud (or Koran) makes about being God's Word is a *false* claim. Which is a polite of saying, in plain, blunt English, the claim is a *lie*. And therefore, to the extent that the pastor could find that my argument was "Talmudical," it was something he could freely and *gladly* reject – as a *falsehood*.

The pastor was *partially* correct in viewing the arguments presented therein as "talmudical." While the bedrock of the claims I make in this book are indeed Biblical – and can be found in *both* the Old and New Testaments – some of the claims presented here do in fact come from the Talmud.

There is nothing I could do about that, even if I wanted to. As you the reader will see, the Talmudical and Biblical claims are intertwined with each other. The Talmudical claims complement and supplement the Biblical claims. The Talmudical claims derive their authority from the Bible. I cannot separate them any more than I can separate the ingredients that go into baked bread.

Sola Scriptura Christians do not believe the

Talmud's claims that it was revealed to Moses at Mt. Sinai orally, and therefore is every bit as much the Word of God as is the written Bible. That being the case, to them, it might therefore follow that the Talmud's claims of being the Word of God are a lie, and therefore, the Talmud must be an *evil* thing. For is not the Talmud's claim a false claim, and therefore a *lie*? And is it not evil to lie?

And now we see why Christians burned talmuds in the Middle Ages. And why my pastor's gut instinct was to reject my arguments. And why Judaism may well have a hard time in convincing the Christian world to walk in the ways of the Seven Laws of the Sons of Noah. For it is a simple fact: *Part* of the arguments of Judaism, in fact, *do* proceed from material found in the Talmud, which lies outside the realm of written scripture, which Christianity feels perfectly at liberty to reject. With some Christians, they feel even a *moral obligation* to reject arguments based on such extra-biblical traditions (see Chapter 13 below).

* * *

Knowing all this as I do, I could not accept Rabbi Scholem Ber's advice to just tell the Gentiles that the

Good News of the Seven Laws of the Sons of Noah can be found in the "Holy Torah." I believe that Christians are congenitally unwilling and even unable to accept arguments which they think arise from outside (what they regard to be) the Word of God.

In a sense, I told Scholem Ber, the Christians are like karaite Sadducees who also, (like today's Christians), did not believe in Oral Tradition, but only in that which is written – the Bible itself. And since there is only a limited mention of the Seven Laws in the *written* Old Testament, one therefore cannot expect these non-Jews to respect extra-biblical, purely Jewish sources such as the Talmud.

I also told him (as he already well knew), there exist few written, if any at all, Jewish materials from the First Century, because that was a century or two before the time of Rabbi Yehudah ha-Nasi (Judah the Prince), who began the writing of what, centuries later, finally became the Talmud in its present form. And therefore, I told Rabbi Scholem Ber, if you want to find proof that knowledge of the Seven Laws existed as long as 2,000 years ago, *and in fact were very popular and well-known, far more so than today*, in the days when the Holy Temple still stood, you *may* find this proof, not so much in Jewish sources, but rather *in the **Christian** holy scriptures*. Here, it is the *Christian* scriptures which actually reveal more light on this matter than do the contemporary Jewish sources.

I must admit, few rabbis, including Scholem Ber, are happy to hear this. But what can I say? True is true.

I recently came across a Wikipedia article about the 7 Laws which mentioned this very thing. If one googles "Seven Laws of Noah" (at least one could do so in 2015), one finds this protocol:

https://en.wikipedia.org/wiki/***Seven_Laws_of_No ah***.

This article provides a summary of the case which Judaism makes for the existence of the 7 Laws, but also has a section about how these Laws made their appearance in Acts 15, which is an account of the First Trial of the Apostle Paul before the assembled Jerusalem Mother Church, where they decided to admit Gentiles into the growing Nazarene movement without first requiring them to submit to circumcision and full observance of Mosaic Law. But more about this later.

Anyway, I told Rabbi Scholem Ber that if I were to try to tell a non-Jew that he could find proof of the Seven Laws in the "Holy Torah," the non-Jew would then roll his eyes and reply, "I'm very sorry; I don't wish to be unpleasant, but that simply won't work for me. I'm not a Jew and Judaism is not my religion. Your Talmud and your religion don't bind me, and I have no desire to explore them since I believe that Christianity is superior to Judaism and in fact has replaced your Law and your Talmud. And in fact, your religion is a *defunct* religion, by *my* standards. So if you expect *me* to respect the Seven Laws of the Sons of Noah, can you therefore please kindly tell me, where I may find references to the Seven Laws of the Sons of Noah *in the **written** Old Testament*, a Holy Scripture which I can and *do* accept? For I accept *nothing* that I can't see in my own Bible."

I told Scholem Ber, if you expect non-Jews to respect the Jewish claim about the Noahide Covenant, you *must* show them how *their own scriptures* bear witness to the Seven Laws. I told him, I am able to do this.

At this point, I broke off the discussion with him. But he or any other nice rabbi could say at this juncture, you may find mention of the Seven Laws in Genesis 9:4-6.

Aha! *That* is a *written* scripture, easily found in the Old Testament. It says therein:

> *Only flesh with the life thereof, which is the blood thereof, shall you not eat.*
>
> *And surely your blood of your lives will I require; at the hand of every beast will I require it; and at the hand of man, even at the hand of every man's brother, will I require the life of man.*
>
> *Whosoever sheddeth the blood of man, by man shall his blood be shed, for in the Image of God made He Man.*

2 COMMANDS

This is progress. We clearly see that God did in fact give commandments to Noah and his sons, which was part of the Covenant which God established with Noah and his sons.

However, the text mentions only two commandments. One of them is a commandment about not eating of the flesh of a living animal, and its blood. Now, one might suppose, surely the animal whose flesh I'm eating is no longer alive, but the implication therefore is, I may not eat the flesh of the limb of an animal which I tore off that animal while it was still alive.

And of course the other commandment is one that bans murder.

These two commandments are in fact two of the Seven Laws, as Judaism reckons the Seven Laws. And the first of the two, in Genesis 9:4, is *extremely* important because, as we will see, the leaders of the Jerusalem Church, as recorded several times in *Acts of the Apostles*, make mention of this very commandment.

But where are the other five commandments?

Our nice rabbi could say, please trust me; they do exist. But this might not be even necessary because, oddly enough – and this again actually might displease our dear rabbi! – we can find also mention of some of the remaining five commandments *in the Christian scriptures.*

As I already said, the very best proof that the Seven Laws of the Sons of Noah lived in the hearts and souls of many, *many* believers – Jewish *and* Christian alike – at the time of Jesus Christ in the First Century, and during the time before the Temple fell, can be found, not in Jewish sources (of which there are very few from the 1st Century), *but rather in the **Christian** scripture known as* Acts of the Apostles!

In Judaism, Jews of course worship under the Abrahamic / Mosaic Covenant, which doesn't apply to non-Jews, and which is why non-Jews have no obligation to keep kosher or perform circumcision, etc. Judaism holds that with the Seven Laws of the Sons of Noah, non-Jews have their own Covenant with God anyway, and therefore don't need the Covenants of Abraham and Moses. Because Noah and his sons, by definition, are the progenitors of the entire human race, it therefore follows that any Covenant which God made with them and their descendants is certainly binding on all mankind.

Judaism holds that, because non-Jews already have a Covenant with God, with which they can be "justified" or "saved," it is therefore unnecessary for them to follow the stricter Covenant of Moses. (This point eluded the Apostle Paul – but more about that later.). The Apostle Peter himself spoke very eloquently in Acts 15 to the difficulties of following the Mosaic Law. But the other Covenant, the Seven Laws of the Sons of Noah, is far simpler, and if a non-Jew but observes only these Seven Laws, this alone is enough for him (though not for a Jew) to earn and enjoy his Heavenly award.

It is for this reason that Judaism seeks no converts to Judaism, because the Gentiles don't need it, since they can "save" themselves without it.

However, Judaism also believes that it is very important to teach the non-Jews about the Noahide Covenant, *and to convert them from paganism to this Covenant.*

* * *

All one needs is to learn how to recognize such evidence when one encounters it in certain of the Christian scriptures. So therefore, I invite one and all to accompany me – "Come and hear," as is a common saying in the Talmud – as we learn more about the Seven Laws of the Sons of Noah, and how these Seven Laws affected the polemic which we find in and in certain other Gospel passages. Come and hear with me, and you will learn things about the original Jerusalem Church, the very origins of the Christian religion which, I am *very* certain, few or none of you ever before realized.

2) THE OLD COVENANT(S) AND THE NEW COVENANT

What is a *"Covenant"*?

A *Covenant* is an *agreement*, a *deal*, a *contract*, a *treaty*, between two or more parties.

In a *Covenant*, both parties promise to do or not do certain things, and have a right to expect certain services or rights from the other party or parties in exchange.

It is a teaching of Christianity that God established a Covenant with Abraham and his descendants, and when Jesus came, he replaced (and even abrogated) this Old Covenant, which only applied to Jews, with a *new Covenant*, which applied to everybody. Every Christian who sees these words knows and understands this, and I need not take pains to prove it.

(Actually, as we will see, according to the Apostle Paul, when God established this New Covenant, the Old, Abrahamic Covenant, which even Paul admitted *had* applied to the Jews, no longer applied for anybody, not even for the Jews, so even Jews were no longer subject to Mosaic Law – according to Paul.)

There are of course in the Old Testament many references to God's old Covenant with the Israelites. One example should suffice:

It is written in the Book of Exodus 2:24:

> *And God heard their groaning, and God remembered His* **Covenant** *with Abraham, Isaac, and Jacob.*

This Abrahamic Covenant is discussed at length in Genesis 15 and 17.

But – *this is neither the first nor the only Covenant which is mentioned in the Pentateuch.*

It is written in Genesis 6:18:

> *But I will establish My* **Covenant** *with thee; and thou shalt come into the ark, thou, and thy sons, and thy wife, and the wives of thy sons with thee.*

And then at greater length in Genesis 9:9-17:

*As for me, behold, I establish My **Covenant** with you, and with your seed after you;*

And with every living creature that is with you, the fowl, the cattle, and with every beast of the earth with you; of all that go out of the ark, even every beast of the earth.

*And I will establish My **Covenant** with you; neither shall all flesh be cut off any more by the waters of the flood; neither shall there be any more a flood to destroy the earth.*

*And God said: This is the token of the **Covenant** with I make between Me and you, and between every living creature that is with you, for perpetual generations.*

*My bow have I set in the cloud, and it shall be for a token of a **Covenant** between Me and the earth.*

And it shall come to pass, when I bring

clouds over the earth, and the bow is seen in the cloud,

*That I will remember My **Covenant** which is between Me and you, and between every living creature of all flesh; and the waters shall no more become a flood to destroy all flesh.*

*And the bow shall be in the cloud, and I shall look upon it, to remember the everlasting **Covenant** between God and every living creature of all flesh that is upon the earth.*

*And God said unto Noah: This is the token of the **Covenant** which I have established between Me and all flesh that is upon the earth.*

* * *

There are *two **Covenants*** mentioned in the Old Testament. The second *Covenant*, the one between God, and Abraham and his descendants, is not binding on non-Jews, but the *first Covenant*, the *Covenant* between God, and Noah and his three sons and their descendants, *is* binding on all who live because, by definition, Noah's three sons are the progenitors of all human beings.

3) WHAT ARE THE SEVEN LAWS OF THE SONS OF NOAH?

Before we may consider what they mean and how they affected certain passages from the New Testament, and how to recognize them when we see them, we first must know what the Seven Laws are.

Here is how the Seven Laws are listed in *Sanhedrin 56a*, from the Babylonian Talmud:

1. Justice. Mankind must build courts of law, with which to administer justice.
2. Blasphemy. One may not level a curse against God. And when one takes an oath before God, to tell the truth, the whole truth, and nothing but the truth, one may not break this oath. In effect, this commandment prohibits lying, especially when God Himself is called to support the lie.
   This law of course supports the integrity of the courts which Law 1 obliges us to erect.
3. Idolatry. One may not worship false gods, but instead only the One, True God.
4. Illicit intercourse. One may not commit adultery, incest, sodomy, or bestiality.
5. Homicide. One may commit neither murder nor suicide.

6. Theft. One may not take goods which belong to others.

7. Limb of a living creature. One may not take the limb from an animal while it lives, and eat that limb. There are variants of this commandment which include prohibitions against eating the blood of an animal. As we will see, this last commandment, with this final interpretation, for our purposes, will be the most important of the Seven Laws, for it is the key to unlocking certain mysteries contained in Acts of the Apostles.

One can easily see how much overlap there is between the Seven Laws of the Sons of Noah and the Ten Commandments. The similarities are obvious. Both sets of laws forbid idolatry, blasphemy (which includes oath-breaking), murder, thievery, and forbidden relationships.

* * *

There may actually exist a kernel of evidence that the Seven Laws were followed by mankind shortly after the Great Flood.

We all have heard of the very ancient (and, admittedly sometimes brutal) *Code of Hammurabi*. It is the oldest surviving code of law in existence anywhere on earth. Many people believe (however wrongly) that Moses borrowed heavily from this code to create the body of law which we find today in the Pentateuch.

But it may be more a case that both codes of law proceeded from a still earlier code of law which was common to both – the Seven Laws of the Sons of Noah.

In 1948, Philip Biberfeld wrote *Universal Jewish History*, and in Volume I, he says, if one breaks down the very name "Hammurabi" etymologically in Hebrew, one comes up with "Ham-rabbi," or "Ham the teacher." Ham was the third son of Noah, and to Biberfeld this was evidence that Hammurabi learned about the Seven Laws of the Sons of Noah from Ham, and built and constituted his Code of Law from them.

We will next look at the first of the Seven Laws.

4) THE FIRST LAW – JUSTICE

The First Law is a very strange one – to erect courts of law.

It is strange, because most if not all other Commandments in the Bible concern themselves with the obligations one personally has between oneself and God. But *this* Law cannot be seen in any individual light, because no single individual can build a body of law (*corpus juris*) only for himself, or by himself. Law-building is a community venture, not something any individual can do for himself.

And moreover, consider that the Seven Laws of the Sons of Noah are, in a Biblical sense, the oldest of all laws. Therefore, the Commandment to erect courts of law is the all-time First of All Laws. *All* laws everywhere proceed from *this* Law! It is, to paraphrase what the late Saddam Hussein once predicted about the coming Gulf War of 1991, "the Mother of All Laws."

Consider now the Ten Commandments. One of these commandments is a commandment to rest, and avoid "work," on the Sabbath. But what *is* "work"?

What may I do and what may I not do? May I, for example, ignite a fire and prepare a hot meal? May I travel, or cohabit with my spouse? *The written Bible itself doesn't say.*

And adultery and forbidden relationships – am I allowed to marry my first cousin? My aunt – no; the Bible expressly forbids this. But the Bible says nothing about whether I may marry my first cousin. So may I? In Judaism and Islam, the answer is *yes*, but in Christianity, the answer is *no*.

And murder – the Bible forbids it, but what *is* "murder"? If someone attacks me and seeks to kill me, may I use deadly force and kill him first? Or, if a foreign country attacks my country, and my country's army seeks to induct me into its army to defend the country, may I join the army, when it means I will have to kill enemy soldiers?

The Bible doesn't say.

The Bible is only a short document. Its length is finite. But the number of human possibilities is endless and infinite. The Bible therefore can never possibly cover all possible human contingencies.

And that is why the First Law of the Sons of Noah is a Commandment to build courts of law. Because God makes Himself invisible from our daily affairs in order to allow us Free Will. (For who doesn't obey traffic laws when he knows a policeman is watching?) And therefore even He will not directly decide in each and every human event what is right and what is wrong.

In the United States, there is a Constitution. It is relatively short. We also have literally hundreds of thousands, if not millions, of laws. And we have literally millions of court decisions, most, if not all, of which, are recorded in law books. Books with memoranda of these decisions literally fill entire law libraries all over the United States. In American Law, past decisions often help the courts make new decisions in new cases.

But how can this be? The Constitution makes no mention of any need to obey, for example, traffic signals. It is because our Constitution gives us the right to create our own laws concerning matters which are not mentioned in the Constitution, and these laws are valid because they take their authority from the Constitution.

God may be compared to the American Founding Fathers who wrote the American Constitution, which is turn became their "Bible," the foundation for all American laws which were created thereafter, just as the Bible is the foundation for all of Western Civilization's subsequent laws.

There are three stories, and a passage from the Old Testament, which illustrate this point that man co-participates with God and shares with God the task of creating laws for man to live by. One story is from the New Testament, and the other two are from the Jewish rabbinical sources. First, the New Testament:

From Matthew 16:15–19:

> *He saith unto them: "but whom say ye that I am?"*

> *And Simon Peter answered and said, "Thou art the Christ, the Son of the Living God."*

> *And Jesus answered and said unto him "Blessed art thou, Simon Bar-Jona, for flesh and blood hath not revealed it to thee, but my Father which is in*

Heaven.

*"And I say also unto thee, that thou art
Peter, and upon this rock I will build
my church, and the gates of Hell shall
not prevail against it.*

*"And I will give unto thee the keys of
the kingdom of Heaven,* **and
whatsoever thou shalt bind on earth
shall be bound in Heaven; and
whatsoever thou shalt loose on earth
shall be losed in Heaven."**

Jesus gave Peter this right, not as a dictator, but as
a chief judge of a law court. ("Peter" is a pun. In
Greek, "petros" means "rock," as in "<u>petro</u>leum," oil
from a <u>rock</u>. In effect, Jesus was saying, "You,
Simon, are a rock – 'Peter' – and upon this rock –
'Peter' – I will build my church.")

For example: In Biblical Judaism (and also
Islam), all statues are forbidden as graven images.
However, since Peter and his successors decided to
change this law and allow statues into Christian
houses of worship, and had a right given them by
Jesus their founder to do so, in Christian doctrine,

their act is recognized in Heaven, according to the above passage, and therefore there is no sin if Christian churches have these "graven images."

* * *

COURTS

"Whatsoever thou shalt bind on earth shall be bound in Heaven; and whatsoever thou shalt loose on earth shall be losed in Heaven" – this same principle can be found in the Old Testament as well:

> *"And it shall come to pass in that day, that I will call My servant Eliakim the son of Hilkiah;*
>
> *And I will clothe him with thy robe, and strengthen him with thy girdle, and I will commit the government into his hand; and he shall be a father to the inhabitants of Jerusalem, and to the House of Judah.*
>
> ***And the key of the House of David will I lay upon his shoulder, so he shall open, and none shall shut; and he shall shut, and none shall open.*** *And I will fasten him as a nail in a*

sure place" (Isaiah 22:20-23).

* * *

And now, in the Talmud:

> *Rabbi Eliezer ben Hyrcanus declared that if a certain oven were made, not in one piece, but in tiles, and if sand were placed in between the tiles, the oven was clean, but the other rabbis said no.*
>
> *Then Rabbi Eliezer brought forth every argument he could think of, but the others didn't accept them. He said to them, "If the* halachah *(the Law) agreed with him, then let this carob-tree prove it!" And the carob-tree was torn 100 cubits out of its roots.*
>
> *Then the other rabbis said, "No proof may be brought from a carob-tree."*
>
> *Then he said, "If the* halacha *agrees with me, let the stream of water prove it!" And the stream of water flowed*

backwards.

But the other rabbis said, "No proof may be brought from a stream of water."

Then Rabbi Eliezer said, "If the halacha *agrees with me, let the walls of this schoolhouse prove it!"*

And the walls began to fall. But Rabbi Joshua rebuked the walls, saying, "When scholars are engaged in a halachic *dispute, what right have you to interfere?" And the walls didn't fall down, to honor Rabbi Joshua, but neither did the walls stand upright again, in order to honor Rabbi Eliezer, and to this day they remain so.*

Then Rabbi Eliezer brought in his biggest gun, his "Big Bertha," in a manner of speaking. He said, **If the** halacha **(the law)** *agrees with me, let it be proved from Heaven!"*

And then an *amazing* thing happened.

God Himself actually heard Rabbi Eliezer and responded!

> *A Heavenly Voice called out, "Why do*
> *you dispute with Rabbi Eliezer, seeing*
> *that in all matters the* halacha *agrees*
> *with him?"*

And then *something else* happened that was even *more* amazing!

> Rabbi Joshua arose and cried, *"Not so;*
> ***it is NOT in Heaven!"***

It makes one's jaw drop. Rabbi Joshua had the nerve *to argue with God Himself*! (Which reminds me of a play which once appeared on Broadway in New York City: *Arms Too Short to Box with God.*)

> *And Rabbi Jeremiah added, "Because*
> *the Law has already been given at Mt.*
> *Sinai, we now pay **no attention** to any*
> *Heavenly Voice, because **You***
> ***Yourself, O God**, wrote in the Law a*
> *long time ago, 'One must incline with*

a majority' (Exodus 23:2)."

And then *the most amazing thing of all happened!*

> *Rabbi Nathan then encountered Elijah
> the Prophet* (who, because he never
> died, frequently appeared to the rabbis
> of the Talmud), *and asked him, "What
> did the Holy One, Blessed be He, do at
> that moment?"*

> *And Elijah the Prophet said, "HE
> LAUGHED WITH JOY, SAYING,
> 'THIS DAY HAVE MY SONS
> DEFEATED ME; THIS DAY HAVE
> MY SONS DEFEATED ME!'"*

> *And all the things which Rabbi Eliezer
> had said were clean, were brought to a
> fire and burned* (Babylonian Talmud
> Baba Metziah, 59b–60a).

* * *

In this story, God and Rabbi Eliezer were correct, and the other rabbis were *wrong*. Nevertheless, their *wrongful* opinion became law, because they had a right to be wrong, a right which came from God, and even God Himself could not change that.

And God *laughed*! *For joy!* He had the same joy that *any* parent has when his children grow up and learn to behave with intelligence and maturity.

The rabbis had the same God-given right to alter law as Peter had – "*And whatsoever thou shalt bind on earth shall be bound in Heaven; and whatsoever thou shalt loose on earth shall be losed in Heaven.*"

Rabbi Jeremiah above said this was because of the Law which God gave on Mt. Sinai, and that is correct – but what he also *could* have said was, this is because of the very first of all laws, which God gave, not only to Israelites, but to all of mankind after the Great Flood.

And one more example, also from the Talmud:

* * *

Once there was a dispute between a minority and majority of rabbis about how to calculate the proper day on which to observe Yom Kippur (the Day of Atonement).

Rabbi Gamliel (the grandson of the Rabbi Gamliel who is mentioned in *Acts of the Apostles 5*, as we will see), *sent a message to Rabbi Joshua, ordering him to report to Rabbi Gamliel, carrying both his walking stick and his money* (which are activities which are forbidden on *Yom Kippur*) *on that very day which he calculated to be* Yom Kippur.

Rabbi Akiva went to Rabbi Joshua and found him very distressed, and said to him, "From the Scripture, I can tell you that whatever Rabbi Gamliel does is correct, for it is written, 'These are the appointed seasons of the LORD, even holy convocations, which ye shall proclaim in their appointed season' (Lev. 23:4).

"Whether in their proper season or not, I know of no other set feasts save these."

Previously, Rabbi Dosa ben Harkinas had also disagreed with Rabbi Gamliel's decision, and Rabbi Joshua went to Rabbi Dosa and said to him, "If we begin to question the lawfulness of the decisions which proceed from Rabbi Gamliel's court, we will also need to question the decision of every court decision from the time of Moses to this day."

Therefore he waited until that day which he believed to be the correct Day of Atonement. On that day he then picked up his walking-stick and carried money (gross violations of *Yom Kippur), and traveled to Rabbi Gamliel, who was in Yavneh.*

Rabbi Gamliel stood up and kissed his cheek, and said, "Come in peace, my master and my disciple!" "My master" in wisdom, and "my disciple" in obedience, in that he accepted Rabbi Gamliel's words (Rosh HaShanah, 2.9).

* * *

As conclusion to this chapter, I note that I originally wrote a draft version of this work a few years before the year 2015, but in that year, I revised this work to make it fit for its final, publication appearance.

And while I was in the process, I came across an interesting article which Catholic Cardinal Timothy Dolan of New York wrote for the Labor Day, September 7, 2015 edition of *The New York Post*.

He was writing about the extensive renovations which his paid laborers had been making to St. Patrick's Cathedral. He compared their labor to how mankind and the work of mankind amounts to co-creation, in a partnership with God Himself, of the beautiful world which He created and which we improve.

He wrote,

> *For Catholics, the greatest prayer is the Mass. At the offertory...we priests borrow a touching prayer from the Jewish meal ritual as we hold up "the*

bread which we offer You...work of human hands...to become for us the bread of life:" "the wine we offer you, work of human hands...to become our spiritual drink.

Almighty God takes "the work of human hands" and consecrates them! That He does with our labor.

And remember: You're all building a cathedral.

And indeed, much more than a mere building, as I'm sure Cardinal Dolan himself would agree – we are building an entire world!

And the basis of the physical objects we build are the laws which we enact to govern ourselves.

* * *

The Laws of God are like any country's constitution. They are both only skeletons and beginnings. And skeletons do not breathe or live.

In order for God's Laws to live, and not be dusty,

old dead bones, Man must act as God's Partner, and add flesh and life to God's skeleton.

And in all of this, Mankind is no mindless slave to God's Laws, but rather is a thinking, free *partner* of God's. We, the human race, are not only God's children, *but are also His co-Creators. God and we create together! We assist God in continually creating our own beautiful world!*

It is an *awesome* and wonderful privilege and responsibility.

> *"And God saw every thing that He had made, and, behold, it was very good..."* (Genesis 1:31).

That is why the First Law of the Sons of Noah is so important, and why it truly is the Mother of All Laws.

5) THE 7th AND LAST OF THE SEVEN LAWS OF THE SONS OF NOAH

The 7th and final of the Seven Laws of the Sons of Noah is the one which is the most crucial to unlocking the secrets in Acts of the Apostles and other Christian passages below. But before we look at the 7th and last of the Seven Laws, it will be well to look at Laws 2 – 6, and compare them to their counterparts in the Ten Commandments of Moses.

* * *

Noahide Law 2: Blasphemy. One may not level a curse against God. And when one takes an oath before God, to tell the truth, the whole truth, and nothing but the truth, one may not break this oath. In other words, this commandment prohibits lying, especially when God Himself is called to support the lie.

Compare this with these commandments from the

Ten Commandments:

> *Thou shalt not take the Name of the Lord thy God in vain; for the Lord will not hold guiltless, him that taketh His Name in vain* (Exodus 20:7). This is a prohibition against Perjury, since one takes oaths on God's Name.

and

> *Thou shalt not witness against thy neighbor, as a false witness* (Exodus 20:13).

* * *

Noahide Law 3: Idolatry. One may not worship false gods, but instead only the One, True God.

In comparison with the Ten Commandments:

> *Thou shalt have no other gods before Me.*

Thou shalt not make unto thee a graven image, nor any manner of likeness (of anything) that is in the heaven from above, or that is in the earth from beneath, or that is in the water from under the earth.

Thou shalt not bow down unto them, nor serve them, for I the Lord thy God am a jealous God, visiting the iniquity of the fathers upon the children, upon the third and fourth generation of them that hate Me,

And showing mercy unto the thousandth generation of them that love me, and keep My commandments (Exodus 20:3–6).

* * *

Noahide Law 4: Illicit intercourse. One may not commit adultery, incest, sodomy, or bestiality.

In comparison with the Ten Commandments:

Thou shalt not commit adultery,

and

Thou shalt not covet thy neighbor's wife (Exodus 20:13–14).

* * *

Noahide Law 5: Homicide. One may commit neither murder nor suicide.

In comparison with the Ten Commandments:

Thou shalt not kill (Exodus 20:13).

* * *

Noahide Law 6: Theft. One may not take goods which belong to others.

In comparison with the Ten Commandments:

Thou shalt not steal,

and

Thou shalt not covet thy neighbor's house...nor his man-servant, nor his maid-servant, nor his ox, nor his ass, nor anything that is thy neighbor's (Exodus 20:13–14).

* * *

To those Christians who believe that the Ten Commandments are a code of law which is universally binding upon all mankind, and who may feel surprised and perhaps also maybe even a little bit offended to learn that Judaism does not believe this, and moreover says that the Ten Commandments do not bind non-Jews – they should therefore take comfort to see that the Seven Laws of the Sons of Noah overlap, for the most part, all the requirements of the Ten Commandments, so by observing the

Seven Laws instead of the Ten Commandments, they are still following their beloved Ten Commandments anyway.

The sole exception is the requirement in the Decalogue to observe the Sabbath Day. There is no requirement in the Seven Laws for any Sabbath observance. But this is not a major hurdle. With the exception of the 7th Day Adventists, there are very few Christians indeed who observe the 7th day of the week as their Sabbath; virtually all Christians have adopted Sunday as their day of rest.

*   *   *

And so now we come to the 7th and final of the Seven Laws of the Sons of Noah – the commandment not to eat the flesh of an animal's limb torn from the animal while it was still alive.

One may not cruelly torture animals, but instead must treat them with mercy, even when, or even especially when slaughtering them for their consumable flesh.

In Judaism, there are differing opinions about what this means, and all of them may be more or less correct.

For example, in Judaism, one may never eat meat and dairy products (such as butter) together, because in Biblical times, the pagans who served Moloch offered sacrifices to Moloch by taking milk from a mother sheep, and taking that mother's lamb and boiling that lamb in the milk taken from its own mother. To the Jews, this was unspeakably cruel.

Because we should treat animals kindly, we ought not slaughter a calf on the same day we also slaughter its mother.

If we take the chicks from a bird, we should let the mother fly away free – "as free as a bird, *vogelfrei*," as Martin Luther put it.

Even if another animal had torn the limb from its victim while it was still alive, one should not eat of it.

Very important note! In a beraisa to the Talmud tractate Sanhedrin 57, Rabbi Chanania ben Gamliel said, **"One may also not eat of the blood taken from a living animal"!**

We will soon enough see how this *beraisa*, or at least the same thinking which caused this beraisa, was used in Acts of the Apostles. Because, and in **conclusion**: *We now know that eating blood from an animal can constitute a known violation of the 7th Law of the Sons of Noah.*

Therefore, when we now see references to the consumption of blood in the New Testament, *we can and will recognize them for what they were, and are: references to the Seven Laws of the Sons of Noah!*

6) THE GOOD CENTURION

And when Jesus was entered into
Capernaum, there came unto him a
(Roman) *centurion, beseeching him,*

And saying, "Lord, my servant lieth at home sick of the palsy, grievously tormented."

And Jesus answered and said unto him, "I will come and heal him."

The centurion answered and said, "Lord I am not worthy that thou shouldest come under my roof; but speak the word only, and my servant shall be healed."

For I am a man under authority, having soldiers under me, and I say to this man, 'Go,' and he goeth, and to another 'Come,' and he cometh, and to my servant, 'Do this,' and he doeth it.

When Jesus heard it, he marvelled, and said to them that followed, "Verily, I say unto you, I have not found so great faith, no, not in Israel." (Matthew 8:5–10).

But Luke's version is better:

And a certain centurion's servant, who was dear to him, was sick, and ready to die.

And when he heard of Jesus, he sent unto him the elders of the Jews, beseeching him that he would come and heal his servant.

And when they came to Jesus, they besought him instantly, saying, "That he was worthy for whom he should do this:

"For he loveth our nation, and he hath built us a synagogue."

Then Jesus went with them. And when he was now not far off from the house, the centurion sent friends to him, saying unto him, "Lord, trouble not thyself, for I am not worthy that though shouldest enter under my roof.

"Wherefore neither thought I myself

worthy to come unto thee, but say in a
word, and my servant shall be healed"
(Luke 7:2–7).

There are a number of questions.

The first question is, *who is this centurion?*

Neither evangelist says so, but it's extremely likely that this is the selfsame Centurion Cornelius, who is mentioned by name in *Acts of the Apostles 10*. Luke after all wrote that work as well as his gospel, so as the evangelist who wrote the Gospel of Luke, he surely knew of Cornelius the Centurion.

When we get to Acts of the Apostles 10, we will see why this Cornelius was almost certainly a convert to Judaism – not a full convert however, but rather a convert to Noahide Judaism – a follower of the Covenant of the Seven Laws of the Sons of Noah.

But for now, we may infer several things about this centurion in the Gospels.

a) He was a *retired* centurion. The Gospels say he lived in Capernaum. But the Roman legions which garrisoned Judea were headquartered at

Caesarea Maritima, which is on the Mediterranean seacoast. Capernaum is in Galilee, a few dozen miles from Caesarea. Centurions on active duty could not possibly maintain villas dozens of miles from their duty posts. But retired centurions could live anywhere they liked.

b) This centurion was evidently wealthy. He had a villa. He had servants (slaves, actually). He had enough money to build an entire synagogue for the local Jews.

c) At this time in history, centurions served at least 25 years on active duty. Most men joined the legions when they turned 17 years of age. So this centurion was at least 42 years old. However, from the passages we may infer that he had been securely established in Capernaum for several years. One does not build a villa, acquire servants, and build a synagogue for local Jews, all overnight. So it is therefore safe to assume this centurion was at least in his mid to late '40's.

Luke himself proves that the centurion in his gospel was some kind of convert to Judaism.

Consider: *This centurion was a Roman officer!* He

represented the hated Roman Empire! An empire whose officials, virtually without exception, looted and stole as much as they possibly could from their subjugated lands, and against whom, *twice*, in the following century, did the desperate Jews rise up in desperate, suicidal revolt, because the Romans were so intolerable.

But Luke says that the local Jews *loved **this Centurion***. Luke said this Centurion *was worthy* of a visit from Jesus. He said this Centurion *had much love* for the Jews, and had even *built a synagogue* for these Jews!

Question: *What kind of Roman officer loves Jews so much that he even builds a synagogue for them??*

More questions: Who were these "elders of the Jews" whom this Centurion was able to summon, and send on his private errand to Jesus? Bach's *St. Matthew's Passion* cites Matthew 27:1 thusly: "When the morning was come, all the chief priests *and the elders of the people* (Pharisees) took counsel together to put him to death." Surely these elders in Capernaum who loved their centurion must also have been Pharisees (which tells us – as we will again shortly see from *Acts* – that the Pharisees were not at all, as a class, necessarily against Jesus, despite the Gospels' best attempts to depict the Pharisees in this light). How was it that a *Roman Centurion* was able to command such service from these elders?

As we will see when we arrive at Acts of the Apostles 10, Jews at this time were required to refrain from contact with Gentiles. This wasn't racist, but instead was required because Gentiles – mostly, anyway – were pagans, and possessed idols. It was idols which Jews had to avoid, not Gentiles per se. However, in Luke's Gospel, Jews freely could and did meet with our Gentile Centurion without breaking any Law.

It can only be that our Centurion was no pagan.

He therefore *must have been a Jew*. Or at least some kind of follower of The One True God. How otherwise could the local Jewish elders have held him in such high esteem?

What *kind* of Jew? Converts to Judaism come in two flavors, the full-blown converts, and the converts to the Covenant of Noah, which is much less strict and demanding.

It is difficult to imagine that our Centurion was himself a full Jew, fully converted to Judaism, because that would have made it impossible for him to function as a Centurion. But we also know he was no pagan to be shunned by Jews, because the Jews of Capernaum revered him and flocked to him. He was even able to request services of them. It can therefore only be that he was a Noahide convert to Judaism, a convert in the second class, not bound by Mosaic Law, but instead bound by God's Covenant for all people – the Seven Laws of the Sons of Noah. And anyway, soon enough we will see testimony from Acts of the Apostles attesting to the fact that Jews and Greeks freely mingled together in synagogues on the Sabbath – despite the general ban forbidding fraternization between Jews and Gentiles, as mentioned by the Apostle Peter in Acts 10.

7) CORNELIUS THE GOOD CENTURION

The easiest thing to do is simply quote the story of Cornelius the Good Centurion from Acts of the Apostles 10. I will also insert my own comments occasionally.

* * *

There was a certain man in Caesarea called Cornelius, a centurion of the band called the Italian band (a

Roman, in other words).

A devout man, AND ONE THAT FEARED GOD with all his house, which gave much alms to the people, and prayed to God always...

(This is, as we say in the USA, a "smoking gun," the evidence that clinches the case, that *proves* Cornelius was a Noahide convert, of the second class, to Judaism. In the Talmud, the expression "God-fearer" means, a Gentile who converted to Noahide Judaism and who follows the Seven laws of the Sons of Noah. Furthermore, donation of money to charity is always praiseworthy in Judaism, as is praying to God continually.

(By the way, attention again should be given to this man's means. Cornelius, and the Centurion from the *Gospel of Luke* [who all but certainly is the same Cornelius] are both very wealthy. In Luke's gospel, the Centurion is wealthy enough to build a synagogue. Above, he is wealthy enough to give alms continuously. In both accounts, the Centurions also have servants.

(He also could not have been a centurion on

active duty in any legion. He appears to have been much too wealthy, and to have had far too much free time. Again, as was true of the Good Centurion in the Gospels, most likely Cornelius was older, served his 25 years in the legions, became wealthy in the process, and retired, so he could live in luxury – *in Saus und Braus* as they say in German -- and leisure by the seaside.)

> *...And now send men to Joppa, and call for one Simon, whose surname is Peter.*
>
> *He lodgeth with one Simon a tanner, whose house is by the seaside: He shall tell thee what thou oughtest to do.*
>
> *And when the angel which spake unto Cornelius was departed, he called two of his household servants, and a devout soldier of them that waited on him continually.*

(Not only does Cornelius have civilian servants; he also even has servants who are, or were, soldiers, who probably served beneath Cornelius in the legions.)

And when he had declared all these things unto them, he (Cornelius) sent them to Joppa...

...And he (Peter) became very hungry, and would have eaten, but while they made ready, he fell into a trance.

And saw Heaven opened, and a certain vessel descending unto him, as it had been a great sheet knit at the four corners, and let down to the earth:

Wherein were all manner of four-footed beasts of the earth, and wild beasts, and creeping things, and fowls of the air.

And there came a Voice to him, "Rise, Peter, kill, and eat."

But Peter said, "Not so, Lord; for I have never eaten any thing that is common or unclean."

And the Voice spake unto him again the second time, "What God hath cleansed, that call not thou common."

This was done thrice: And the vessel was received up again into Heaven...

(Most Christians believe that this scene is the first sign of Christianity's eventual breakaway from Mosaic Law, that here, the early Christians now had a free hand to ignore Mosaic Law restrictions on one's diet. But no – this entire passage is nothing more than analogy. This vision really had nothing to do with whether Peter literally should or should not eat unclean food. Rather, the point of the vision is to compare the eating of forbidden foods to association with forbidden Gentiles. The point of this vision is whether Peter should now associate with Gentiles.

(And for this reason, the Voice's response was irrelevant to the issue at hand – should Peter meet Cornelius? Because, for reasons already established, we know that Cornelius was *not* unclean, and that Peter could already associate with him – and Peter could or should have known this too – without violation of Mosaic Law, since Cornelius was *not* a pagan to whom this was forbidden. And furthermore, we shall see that Jews had frequent and abundant contact with Gentiles during this period – *if* they were Noahide converts.

(Really, the Voice *should* simply have told Peter that his fears were groundless, since Cornelius was a "God-fearer," not a pagan, and therefore wasn't unclean.)

> *...Then Peter went down to the men which were sent unto him from Cornelius, and said, "Behold, I am he whom ye seek. What is the cause wherefore ye are come?*
>
> *And they said, "Cornelius the Centurion,* **a just man AND ONE THAT FEARETH GOD and of good report among the Jews***, was warned from God by a holy angel to send for thee into his house and to hear words of thee."*

(Again, Cornelius is called "a just man," *and* a "*God-fearer.*" Which, again, *proves* that he was a Noahide covert to Judaism, a convert who was *not* required to observe all of Mosaic Law, since the

Covenant to which he'd converted was not the Covenant which God made with Abraham and his descendants, but rather the Covenant of the Seven Laws of the Sons of Noah.)

> *Then called he them in, and lodged them. And on the morrow Peter went away with them, and certain brethren from Joppa accompanied him.*

> *And on the morrow after they entered into Caesarea. And Cornelius waited for them, and had called together his kinsmen and near friends.*

> *And as Peter was coming in, Cornelius met him and fell down at his feet, and worshipped him.*

(This is exaggeration. It is flatly impossible, and even ridiculous. Cornelius was a "God –fearer" – according to Luke's own words – and no man may both fear God, and also worship another human being, or any being other than the One, Living, True God.

(Furthermore, even if a Christian were to claim

that Peter or any other Christian "worshipped" Jesus himself as the Son of God, that description can apply, at most, to and only to Jesus himself. No Christian can claim that Peter or Cornelius could conceivably have "worshipped" any person other than Jesus.

(Indeed, many Protestants decry the Roman Catholic veneration of the Blessed Virgin Mary, saying that praying to her is the same thing as worshippng her, and not even she, as the mother of Jesus himself, is entitled to that.

(Luke has *definitely* exaggerated the true situation.

(I wish I could understand and read Greek, so I could see for myself what verb Luke actually used. However, I know German and can read Dr. Martin Luther in his original German, and he knew Greek, and translated the New Testament from Greek, and the verb Luther used was "*anbeten*," which means "worship." And King James' eminent scholars in London almost a century later, who also knew Greek, translated the New Testament into English, and they too used the verb "worship." I can only suppose they all translated Luke properly, and "worship" is actually what Luke – wrongly – meant and wrote.)

But Peter took him up, saying, "Stand up; I myself am also a man."

(*Mais certainement* – but *of course.*)

And as he talked with him, he went in, and found many that were come together.

And he went unto them, "Ye know how that it is an unlawful thing for a man that is a Jew to keep company or come unto one of another nation; but God hath shewed me that I should not call any man 'common' or 'unclean'" (Acts of the Apostles 10:1–2, 5–8, 10–16, 21–28).

(Note how this proves that the issue in Peter's vision was *not at all* whether he should eat unkosher, unclean foods, but rather whether he should associate with Gentiles. For here, Peter says nothing about literal food, but instead explains how his vision has taught him he should now mingle with Gentiles – even, presumably, with *pagan* Gentiles.

(And again, Luke has exaggerated the situation, since Jews in fact *could* freely mingle with uncircumcised "God-fearers," since they weren't pagans. And Luke himself *obviously knew this*, since in his own gospel, cited above, his [Cornelius the] Centurion of Luke 7 was an uncircumcised Gentile "of the Italian band" who freely associated with Jews, was loved by them, and who even built a synagogue for them.)

* * *

When Cornelius met Peter, he already was no pagan, but rather a convert to Noahide Judaism.

8) CONVERTS ON THE FIRST PENTECOST – BUT FROM WHAT RELIGION TO WHAT RELIGION?

And when the day of Pentecost was fully come, they (the Apostles) *were all with one accord in one place* (Acts 2:1).

(Of course. This was the Jewish festival of *Shavuot*, a name which literally means "sevens," since it falls seven full weeks after Passover. It is one of the three *shalas rogalim*, or "pilgrim festivals" [literally, "three feet"], which are mentioned in the Pentateuch as holy days of rest, similar to the Sabbath. *Rogalim* means "feet" in Hebrew, and these festivals were called "the three feet" because it was the Jewish custom for the Jews to walk to Jerusalem and be there for these festivals, as all the gospels say was the case with Passover, when tens of thousands of pilgrims were expected every year. The other two *shalas rogalim* were *Pesach* [Passover], and *Sukkot*, which was an 8-day festival which occurred in early autumn. It was therefore entirely natural for the apostles to gather together on this day of "Pentecost," and not earlier.)

And suddenly there came a sound from heavens as of a rushing mighty wind, and it filled all the house where they were sitting.

And there appeared unto them cloven tongues like as of fire, and it sat upon each of them...

...Then they that gladly received his (Peter's) *word were baptized: and the same day there were added unto them about 3,000 souls"* (Acts of the Apostles 2:2–3, 41).

* * *

The reason there was such a large crowd present who could hear Peter and be converted by him, was because they were in Jerusalem for the same reason Peter and the disciples also were there – they were all Jews, in Jerusalem together to celebrate *Shavuot.*

But now, *earlier* on this day, before Peter ever converted even the first soul to Christianity –

– There was a great crowd of people – Jews,

really – who were gathered outside the room where the Apostles were when they received the tongues of fire, and they heard the Apostles "speaking in tongues."

> *And how hear we every man in our own tongue, wherein we were born?*
>
> *Parthians and Medes, and Elamites, and the dwellers in Mesopotamia and in Judaea, and Cappadocia, in Pontus, and Asia,*
>
> *Phrygia, and Pamphylia, in Egypt, and in the parts of Libya about Cyrene,* **and strangers from Rome, Jews and proselytes,**
>
> *Cretes and Arabians, we do hear them speak in our tongues the wonderful works of God* (Acts of the Apostles 2:8–11).

This text states a number of place-names, and thereby implies that the persons in Jerusalem from these places were of the respective (non-Jewish) nationalities from the places named in Acts. But in fact, these were certainly *Jews* who happened to come from the various places mentioned in the text. Because, Gentiles would have no motivation to congregate *en masse* in Jerusalem to celebrate Jewish festivals – but *Jews* who resided in those lands would have great reason to do so. The same thing happens in Jerusalem to this day; Jews from various nations such as the United States, Great Britain, South Africa, France etc., come to Jerusalem on the occasions of major Jewish holidays such as *Shavuot*, in this case.

First question: *Who are the "strangers from Rome"*?

Note: There are *no* "strangers" from Parthia. Or Media. Or Mesopotamia, or Judea or Cappadocia, Pontus or Asia

There are "strangers" only from Rome – no other place. But what is the difference?

> *And she* (Zipporah) *bore a son, and he* (Moses) *called his name "**GER**shom," for he said: "A **stranger** have I been in a strange land"* (Exodus 2:22).

In Hebrew, *ger* means "stranger" or "foreigner;"

knowing that, it's therefore easy to see why Moses named his son "**GER**schom." And in Judaism there are two kinds of *gerim*, and both describe conversion to Judaism. A *ger tzedek* is a "righteous stranger," literally, and refers to a Gentile who fully converted to Judaism, and takes upon himself to observe all of Mosaic Law, exactly as the most pious of Jews will. A *ger toshav*, literally a "resident alien," is a Gentile who has converted, not to full Judaism, but instead to the Covenant of the Seven Laws of the Sons of Noah. Because he is no pagan, the Bible recognizes his right to live among Jews inside the Holy Land.

*   *   *

The inference is, these "strangers from Rome" were in fact Roman Noahide converts to Judaism.

Second question: *Who were these "proselytes"* (Acts of the Apostles 2:10)?

The English translation uses the word "proselytes," and here the meaning is unmistakable; it means "converts." (And my Polish New Testament uses the word *proselici*, which obviously is a variant of "proselytes." Luther used the word *Einwanderer*, which means, those who wander in, or immigrants.)

*   *   *

There is a charming and heartwarming *parable* (yes – a *parable*; Jesus did not invent this form of moral instruction via story-telling; for many years, the Pharisees had given moral instruction to the Jewish people via parables. Jesus simply followed their long-standing example with *his* parables) – anyway, there is this charming and heartwarming parable found in the holy *Midrash* which illustrates the love and respect that Judaism holds for those Gentiles to convert to full Judaism, a course of action which Judaism does not seek or encourage.

THE KING AND THE STAG

A king had a flock which went out to the fields, and came in again in the evening. So it went every day. One day a stag came in with the flock. He went along with the goats and grazed with them. The king was told, "A stag has joined the flock and is grazing with them every day, going out with them and coming in with them." The king felt love for the stag, and when he saw him going out to the fields, he gave orders, "Let him have good pasture according to his will; no man shall beat him; take great care with him!" And also when the stag came in with the flock, the king would say, "Give him to drink." So he showed the he loved the stage very much.

The king's servants said to him, "My Lord, how many rams are yours; how many sheep are yours; how many goats are yours; yet you give us no special instructions concerning them. Yet about this stag, every day you give us your commands."

Said the king to them, "The flock, whether they want to or not, thus is their way, to graze in the field every day, and in the evening, to come in and sleep in the fold. The stags sleep in the wilderness; it is not their way to enter the places cultivated by men. Shall we not then account it as a merit to this one who has left behind the whole of the broad, vast wilderness, the abode of all the beasts, and has come to stay in the courtyard?"

So God has told us, "Love ye therefore the proselyte." (Deuteronomy 10:19)

Numbers Rabbah 8:2

* * *

But who, or even what, were these *converts*?

It is *impossible* that these converts were converts to Christianity. Note when, and where, this story took place. It was in Acts of the Apostles 2, on the morning of the first Pentecost, when the tongues of flame descended upon the apostles. This was *before* Peter addressed the crowd of people, and *before* he converted the first 3,000 souls to Christianity. At this moment in time, the *only* followers of Jesus were his disciples plus a few women; *there existed as yet **not one single convert to Christianity*** – but there were *already* "converts" in the crowd who heard Peter on that day.

Moreover, the Apostle Paul himself had not yet

begun to preach to the Gentiles, and would not for several more years, and he was the very first Christian leader to preach to Gentiles.

It can *only* be, that these were converts *to Judaism*.

But what kind of converts? Acts of the Apostles doesn't say. Some of them might well have been full converts to Judaism. But many of the rest were certainly converts to the Covenant of the Seven Laws of the Sons of Noah – hence, the "strangers from Rome."

*   *   *

The best evidence for the existence of the Seven Laws of the Sons of Noah in Acts of the Apostles may be found in the account of the two trials of Paul, both of which took place in Jerusalem. But before we can examine these, we first need a bit more background. We need to examine the various places Paul visited in Asia (Minor) and Greece, and see to whom it was that he was preaching, and converting.

9) PAUL PREACHES IN SYNAGOGUES TO JEWS AND GENTILES

There was a growing controversy in the new Nazarene movement whether the new Church should accept Gentile converts and, if it did, should it require of these Gentile followers of Jesus that they first undergo circumcision and become full Jews?

In Acts of the Apostles 10, we've already seen that Peter didn't even want to be in the presence of Gentiles, never mind convert them.

But in Acts of the Apostles 2, we see Peter converting the first 3,000 souls to Christianity, who were in Jerusalem from many places all over what we would now call the Middle East, both from within and without the Roman Empire. But who were they? Were they really Gentiles? Acts 2 certainly implies that.

But when we think about Peter's reluctance in Acts 10, to even permit himself to suffer to be in the mere *presence* of the Gentile Cornelius, someone who moreover was unobjectionable because he was a "God-fear" and *not* a pagan, then Peter's previous *eagerness* to convert 3,000 *pagan*(?) souls to Christianity on the first Pentecost certainly is inexplicable.

Moreover, as we already noted above, the decision whether to accept Gentile converts into the Nazarene movement, as Gentiles, and not as ex-Gentiles who had converted to full-blown Judaism (and who thereafter were as Jewish as any other Jew)

– this decision was still far in the future. The Apostle Paul (as Paul not Saul) himself literally didn't yet even exist, and he was the very first Apostle to the Gentiles.

And what – if Peter *did* accept 3,000 *pagan* converts to Christianity on the first Pentecost – *did he also* **circumcise** *all 3,000 of these converts on the very same day??* Because, until Paul's First Trial, which didn't take place until years later in Acts 15 (in AD 49, according to Jack Finegan in his *Handbook of Biblical Chronology*), circumcision was the requirement for *all* Gentile converts to Christianity. They had to be *first* Jewish and only then could also become Christian. Since it is impossible to circumcise 3,000 men on the same day, and since Peter and his Church didn't yet accept converts without circumcision, it therefore must be that the 3,000 souls whom Peter converted on that first day were *already* Jews. And this counts the "strangers" from Rome as Jews.

And then there are certain hints which Acts 2 furnishes to us.

Why was there a great throng of people who were in Jerusalem to hear Peter speak to them on the first

Pentecost?

We already have our answer. There was already a great throng of *Jews* in Jerusalem on the first Pentecost, because it was already the traditional *Jewish* pilgrim festival of *Shavuot*. On pilgrim festivals, Jews came literally from all over the known world to be in Jerusalem. That is why the Apostles themselves were in Jerusalem.

And Acts 2 also gave us certain specific hints, when it said there were "strangers" from Rome, and *proselytes*, who could *only* have been *Jewish* converts.

On the first Pentecost, Peter converted *no* Gentiles to Christianity. He converted *only* those who were *already* Jewish, who were either born Jewish, or who had converted fully to Judaism, or Noahide converts to Judaism. (I would suppose that in the confusion to baptize 3,000 souls in one day, Peter was unable to take the time to discern whether a given convert were born Jewish, was a full convert, or was a Noahide convert.)

THE EARLY CHRISTIANS PREACHED AND PRAYED, NOT IN SO-CALLED "CHURCHES,"

BUT IN THE GREAT TEMPLE AND
SYNAGOGUES, WHERE THEY WERE
ACCEPTED AND WELCOMED.

> *Now Peter and John went up together*
> ***into the Temple*** *at the hour of prayer,*
> *being the 9th hour.*

(This would be the afternoon service known as
mincha, which may be said anytime after midday
until sunset. Judging from what I have seen at what is
possibly the largest synagogue in Brooklyn, New
York, at 770 Eastern Parkway, Jews probably
wandered in and out of the Great Temple all
afternoon long to recite *mincha*.)

> *And a certain man lame from his*
> *mother's womb was carried, whom*
> *they laid daily **at the gate of the***
> ***Temple which is called Beautiful***, *to*
> *ask alms **of them that entered the***
> ***Temple***.

> *Who seeing Peter and John **about to***
> ***go into the Temple***, *asked for alms...*

> *...And he leaping up stood, and*

walked, **and entered with them into the Temple**, *walking, and leaping, and praising God...*

...And they knew it was he which sat for alms **at the beautiful gate of the Temple**, *and they were filled with wonder and amazement at that which had happened unto him.*

And as the lame man which was healed held Peter and John, all the people ran together unto them **in the porch that is called Solomon's**, *greatly wondering* (Acts of the Apostles 3:1–3, 8, 10–11).

and

...And by the hands of the apostles were many signs and wonders wrought among the people **and they were all with one accord in Solomon's Porch**.

...But the angel of the Lord by night opened the prison doors, and brought

them forth, and said,

"Go, stand and speak in the Temple *to the people all the words of this life."*

And when they heard that, **they entered into the Temple early in the morning,** *and taught…*

…Then came one and told them, saying, "Behold, the men whom ye put in prison **are standing in the Temple,** *and teaching the people"…*

*…****And daily in the Temple,*** *and in every house, they ceased not to teach and preach Jesus Christ* (Acts of the Apostles 5:12, 19–21, 25, 42).

and

And straightaway he (Paul) *preached Christ* **in the synagogues** (of Damascus), *that he* (Jesus) *is the Son of God* (Acts of the Apostles 9:20).

and

And when they (Saul/Paul and Barnabas) *were at Salamis,* **they preached the word of God in the synagogues of the Jews** (Well – whose other synagogues would those have been?) ...

...But when they departed from Perga, they came to Antioch in Pisidia, **and went into the synagogue on the Sabbath day,** *and sat down.*

And after the reading of the law and the prophets, **the rulers of the synagogues sent unto them,** *saying "Ye men and brethren, if ye have any word of exhortation for the people, say on"...*

(The morning synagogue service for Sabbath, then and now, consisted of two portions, *shacharit* and *musaf.* In general, synagogue services were designed to be verbal analogues of the cycle of animal and grain sacrifices at the Great Temple, mimicking those sacrifices verbally, allowing Jews away from the Temple to participate vicariously in the cycle of sacrifices. In the Great Temple, there was an additional sacrifice on Sabbath and Festivals called which was called *musaf*, and this extra service is what the Jews recited in synagogues everywhere on the Sabbath.

(The first portion of the morning service for the Sabbath, *shacharit*, concluded with a cyclical reading from a portion of the Pentateuch, so that the entire Five Books of Moses would be recited over the course of one year. This was called the *Torah* reading, or the Reading of the Law.

(The *haftorah* was/is recited immediately after the *Torah* reading. The *haftorah* reading was/is always a short reading taken from the prophetic works of the Old Testament, whose theme in some way complemented the *Torah* reading. Since this reading concludes the *shacharit* portion of the morning service for Sabbath, then and now, it created a natural break before the *musaf* portion, and an opportunity to let visitors speak.)

> ...(And after Paul and Barnabas'd had their say), *And when the Jews were gone out of the synagogue,* **the Gentiles besought these words might**

> **be preached to them the next Sabbath**" (Acts of the Apostles 13:5, 14–15, 42).

Now what is *this*? In Act 10, we learned that the Jews were supposed to *shun* the Gentiles. Yet here they are, happily allowing the Gentiles to worship The One True God alongside them. Obviously, these can't be pagans. But they're not Jews, either. The only remaining possibility is that they were Noahide converts, who had remained Gentiles even after converting.

and

> *Now when the congregation was broken up* (which means, after the synagogue service was over), *many of the Jews **and religious proselytes** followed Paul and Barnabas: who, speaking to them, persuaded them to continue in the grace of God* (Verse 43).

Who are these "proselytes"? The previous comment applies here too. Paul didn't convert these; they were *already* converted (to – *something*) before

Paul had ever arrived on the scene. They are *not* Jews; the text makes that quite plain that these were neither born Jews nor Jews converted to full Judaism. Here, Luther's translation comes again to the rescue. He refers to these as **"God-fearers"** which, as we already know, is Talmudical shorthand used to refer to Noahide converts.

These therefore can only be Noahide converts to Judaism.

and

And when it came to pass in Iconium, **that they went together into the synagogue of the Jews, and so spake, that a great multitude of both the Jews AND ALSO OF THE GREEKS BELIEVED** (*Acts of the Apostles 14: 1*).

(Question: What were "Greeks" (and, "Gentiles," above, in Salamis) doing in a synagogue? They weren't there to hear Paul and Barnabas; again, they, were *already* there as a matter of long habit. They were also Noahide converts to Judaism.

(This same question applies to the following quote.)

*Now when they had passed through Amphipolis and Apollonia, they came to Thessalanica, **where was a synagogue of the Jews:***

And Paul, as his manner was, went in unto them, and three Sabbath days reasoned with them out of the scriptures...

*...And some of them believed, and consorted with Paul and Silas, **and of the devout Greeks** a great multitude...*

...Now while Paul waited for them at Athens, he spirit was stirred in him, when he saw the city wholly given to idolatry.

Therefore disputed he in the synagogue with the Jews, and with the devout persons (though why would he waste his time and dispute in synagogues with Jews and "devout persons," since they weren't the "idolators" who had so vexed him?) *and in the market* (the *agora*) *daily with them that met with him* (and there follows a long description of Paul's dialogues with members of various pagan Greek schools of thought) (Acts of the Apostles 17:1– 2, 4, 16–17).

(Question: Who were these "devout persons" in the synagogue with the Jews? "Pious persons" is what appears in the King James English version – but here, it is Martin Luther again who actually got this correct, for he twice used the expression *"Gottes-fürchtiger,"* which means, "they who *fear God.*

(Once again – as in Acts 13: 43 above – we have our "smoking gun," our *proof*, because this language is unmistakable. Gentiles who are not pagans, who fear the Only, Living, True God, and serve only Him – these can be nothing other than Noahide converts to Judaism.

and

After these things Paul departed from Athens and came to Corinth...

...And he reasoned in the synagogue every Sabbath, and persuaded the Jews and the Greeks...

...(But evidently not all the Jews, because) *And when they* (the Jews) *opposed themselves, and blasphemed, he shook his raiment, and said unto them, "Your blood be upon your own heads; I am clean: from henceforth I will go unto the Gentiles."*

(What – was Paul *threatening to kill* the Jews?)

And he departed thence, and entered into a certain man's house, named Justus, one that worshipped God, whose house joined hard to the synagogue (Acts of the Apostles 18:1, 4, 6–7).

Once again, the Luther Bible reveals more than does the King James Version.

- In Verse 4 of the King James Version (KJV), Paul "persuaded" Jews and Gentiles to convert to

Christianity – which can mean, he *attempted* to convince these people. But Luther's verb is stronger, and means "convince."

- In Verse 6 of the KJV, Paul declared that henceforth, he would "Go unto the Gentiles." But that can mean pagans or Noahide converts. Luther's translation uses the word "*Heiden*," which can only mean "pagan." (The English word "heathen" derives from the German word *Heiden*.)

(That doesn't make a lot of sense, however, since the first place Paul went to was to the house of this fellow named Justus who, as the text makes clear, was no pagan.)

- In Verse 7, the KJV says only that Justus "worshipped God" (*anbeten*). But Luther's translation says that Justus was a "God-fearer" (*Gottesfürchtiger*). Since we now know that this word is code for "Noahide convert," we therefore know that Justus was a Noahide convert to Judaism. That fact that he built his house adjacent to the local synagogue only further proves the point.

Acts 18 & 19 also mentions that Paul preached in a synagogue in Ephesus, though no Gentiles are mentioned.

10) THE CONTRADICTION – HAS ANYONE SPOTTED IT?

There is a contradiction here.

On the one hand, in Acts 10, Peter says to Cornelius the Gentile,

> *"Ye know how that it is an unlawful thing for a man that is a Jew to keep company or come unto one of another nation."*

But on the other hand, we have seen almost a dozen instances, in two of the four Gospels and in Acts of the Apostles, where Gentiles freely mixed with Jews, who were only very happy to receive them.

In summary, here are the cases:

a) Matthew 8, the story of the Good Centurion.

b) Luke 7, again the story of the Good Centurion, but with more details. According to Luke, the Jews and this man loved each other. This man even built a synagogue for the Jews. And, the

Jews were so much under how influence that he was able to ask Pharisees to go out on the road, meet Jesus, and ask Jesus to come to his home to heal his sick servant.

c) Acts 2, the story of the first Pentecost, when Peter converted the first 3,000 souls to Christianity. But these persons were either all Jews, or Noahide converts, including "strangers from Rome" and "proselytes" who, however, *had* to have been Noahide converts to Judaism, since they were not themselves full Jews, and since at this point there were *no* converts yet to Christianity, but these were *already* "converts." The *only* possibility which fits all the given facts is that these were already Gentiles who'd converted to Noahide Judaism.

d) Acts 13 reports that Saul/Paul and Barnabas preached in a synagogue in Salamis (Greece) to both Jews and Gentiles who, because they attended Sabbath services at the synagogue, must have been Noahide converts.

e) In Acts 14, Paul and Barnabas journeyed to Iconium and preached in a synagogue to both Jews and Greeks alike.

f) In Acts 17, Paul and Silas are now in Thessalonica, and again have found a synagogue in which to preach, a synagogue which is filled not only with Jews but with "devout Greeks" (KJV) who, according to Luther's translation, were "God-fearers" and therefore must have been Noahide converts.

g) Also in Acts 17, Paul has traveled to Athens, and the same thing happens – he finds a synagogue which serves not only Jews but also Noahide converts. In fact, *it seems harder to find a synagogue **without** Noahide converts than it to find one **with** Noahide converts.*

h) And finally, in *Acts 18*, Paul now travels to nearby Corinth, where he preaches in a synagogue to Jews, but with only partial success. In anger, he lays a pox on their house, announces he will henceforth preach to pagans, and leaves, but only goes a few meters, to the house of Titius Justus, who is no pagan but who instead is a Noahide convert, and whose house abuts the synagogue.

* * *

The evidence is plain. Despite anything Peter may have said to the contrary in Acts 10, Jews in fact were allowed to have contact with Gentiles – and did so often – *if the Gentiles were Noahide converts*.

11) SOMETHING REMARKABLE

In our times, almost nobody except for Jews have ever even heard of the Seven Laws of the Sons of Noah. I have heard of exactly *one* Noahide church on earth, this one in Tennessee.

This is why it's easy for Gentiles to dismiss Jewish claims of the existence of the Seven Laws as just a Jewish fairy tale.

But – in fact, from what we've already seen from the New Testament – and I will shortly discuss the evidence that the Jerusalem Church itself practiced the Covenant of the Seven laws of the Sons of Noah – it is *clear*, that in the later years of the Temple, the Noahide Covenant had *many, many* followers. It was *very* popular and well-known.

So what happened? In a word, "war." War happened. A few years after Paul's Second Trial before the Jerusalem Church, the Great Jewish Revolt of 66 – 73 AD (CE) broke out. At its conclusion, the Great Temple was destroyed, and the Jerusalem Church was no longer in any position to challenge Paul's version of Christianity. Pauline Christianity became the norm for Christianity, which then proceeded to break away from Judaism, which has led to Christianity as we know it today. And all the Noahide converts to Judaism, who looked to Jerusalem for their leadership, simply disappeared.

So what is "remarkable"? Simple – the *fact* that, at one time there were many thousands, perhaps even *millions* of persons who followed the Noahide Covenant.

Exaggeration? I think not. At that time, the Roman Empire had a population of around 70 million, and that doesn't include lands outside the Empire, such as Parthia. I have seen – somewhere, I cannot now recall where – an estimate that at this time, *perhaps 10% of the Roman world was Noahide!* And now, given the evidence we've seen in *Acts of the Apostles*, I can *easily* believe that!

What could have happened, if there had been no Jewish Revolt?

We'll look at that, after we examine Paul's two trials.

12) THE FIRST TRIAL (HEARING) OF THE APOSTLE PAUL

This was not an adversarial affair. Paul was not accused of any wrong-doing – this time. It might be more accurate therefore to call this a "hearing."

The Issue

According to Jack E. Finegan (*Handbook of Biblical Chronology*), the first trial of Paul took place around the year 49 AD (CE).

The specific issue was, must Gentile converts to Christianity first undergo circumcision?

> *And certain men which came down from Judaea taught the brethren, and said, "Except ye be circumcised after the manner of Moses, ye cannot be saved."*

> *When therefore Paul and Barnabas had no small dissension and disputation with them, they determined that Paul and Barnabas, and certain other of them, should go up to Jerusalem unto the apostles and elders*

about this question
(Acts of the Apostles 15:1–2).

"Judaea" is a euphemism which means, the headquarters of the Jerusalem Church in Jerusalem, since Jerusalem was the capital of Judaea.

The issue here is not only circumcision. Circumcision is simply the step that a man must take if he wants to convert to full Judaism. The Jews did not (and still don't) consider a Gentile to be a Jew unless and until he undergoes circumcision., and such a Gentile is not obligated to observe Mosaic Law unless and until he undergoes circumcision. Really, the demand is, all converts to Christianity must first become *full* Jews, and must thereafter observe all the Mosaic Laws, just like any other born Jew, before the Jerusalem Church will accept them.

However, Noahide converts *never* had to undergo circumcision as a condition to become a Noahide convert, and never afterward had any obligation to observe Mosaic Law – except of course to the extent that Mosaic Law itself incorporates Noahide Law.

* * *

Now Paul has arrived in Jerusalem, and the story continues from Verse 5. — ⫯CTS 15: 5

> *But there rose up certain **of the sect of Pharisees which believed**, saying, that it was needful to circumcise them and to command them to keep the law of Moses.*

I *really* have to interrupt the narrative at this point.

"Pharisees which BELIEVED"??

In other words, those who were *both true Pharisees **and** true followers of Jesus*! Gee – who knew *that* existed?

Do not the Gospels tell us that Jesus was the arch-enemy to the Pharisees, and that the Pharisees were bitter, evil, hypocritical, and implacably, automatically opposed to Jesus? And was not Jesus the anti-Pharisee, preaching a kind, new religion based on love, which the "legalistic, hair-splitting" Pharisees strongly opposed?

A study of the Gospels will certainly show that.

However, even the Gospels (in spite of themselves) give certain hints that this was not totally or always true.

It is a subject which deserves its own book. I won't go into detail here, since that is not the topic of this book; moreover, notable authors such as the late Hyam Maccoby have already done so (and I *highly* recommend his books!).

But I have one thing to say. In Acts 5, Peter goes on trial before the entire Sanhedrin, and one Pharisee named Rabbi Gamliel *defended* Peter, and as a result, Peter was *acquitted* of the accusation against him, since the Pharisees comprised a majority of the Sanhedrin and they all voted to *acquit* Peter.

Acts portrays this Rabbi Gamliel as an ordinary, average, typical Pharisee. But Acts very much understates Gamliel's importance, perhaps deliberately. He was no ordinary Pharisee. He was in fact *the leader of the whole Pharisee movement* just, as we've already seen (above in Chapter 4), his own grandson of the same name was in the following century. Both Rabbi Gamliels were held in the highest esteem and respect by their respective parties, who followed the lead of these two men and voted according to the desires of these men. And with their majority they voted to acquit Peter simply because, as Acts 5 shows, Rabbi Gamliel supported Peter, and the rest followed Rabbi Gamliel's lead.

If the Pharisees were so bitterly opposed to Jesus that they sought to put him to death, does it make any sense at all that their leader and their entire movement, only a few short years later, would vote to *acquit Jesus' own chief disciple* when he was accused of similar wrong-doing as Jesus himself?

So perhaps the case against the Pharisees might not be so black as the evangelists describe it. But that's another story for another time and another author. Right now, we're going back to the examination of Paul's first hearing before the Jerusalem Church.

In Verses 7 – 9, Peter argues why their church should convert the Gentiles without circumcision, arguing that God purifies their hearts with "faith" just as He does their own. Verses 10 & 11 go like this:

> *"Now therefore why tempt ye God, to put a yoke upon the neck of the disciples, which neither our fathers*

nor we were able to bear?

"But we believe that through the grace of the Lord Jesus Christ we shall be saved, even as they."

Really, if the yoke of Mosaic Law is too much for anybody to bear, Jew and Gentiles together, and if, through faith in Jesus Christ, Gentile hearts can be made as pure as Jewish hearts, then should not the entire Church *immediately* have abandoned the *entire* Law? But the Jerusalem Church *clearly* did *not* do any such thing, though this is precisely what Paul espoused in his own epistles never, of course, sent to Jerusalem, but rather to various churches of Gentiles where he'd preached and converted.

Then in Verse 12 only, Paul and Barnabas spoke to the multitude. Then in the next verse, St. James began to render his verdict, and this is what primarily concerns us.

Who was St. James? He is "James the Lesser;" the New Testament says he was the brother of Jesus. (There was another James who, according to Acts 12, was martyred by the order of King Herod Agrippa.)

Protestants take this literally, and believe James was Jesus' biological brother. Well, if we accept the Christian claim that God Himself was Jesus' father, and unless we believe that God was James' father too, James could not have been more than Jesus' *half-*brother, with Mary as their common mother, but naturally with different fathers. But in any event, Protestants believe literally that he was Jesus' (half) brother (and that after the "Virgin Birth," Mary his mother led a normal marital life with her husband, and produced more children). Catholics believe that Mary the Mother of Jesus was a virgin her entire life, and therefore never had more than one child, so therefore James could not literally have been Jesus' brother. However, he was certainly related to Jesus, at least as a cousin, so, just as royal dynasties do when a ruler departs (usually by death), his son or nearest relative becomes the next ruler. And that was why and how James became the leader of the Jerusalem Church.

James' words appear in Verses 13 – 29. First he gives general words about the Gentiles as being people of God. Then Verse 19 arrives at the heart of the matter: He agrees with Peter and Paul that the Gentile converts ought not to be forced to bear the yoke of the entire Law.

"Wherefore my sentence is, that we trouble them not, which from the Gentiles are turned to God"

And – ahhh! – *finally* – *now* we arrive at those words of James which are the whole purpose of this entire book! The following words which, as we say in America, are the "money words."

*"But that we write unto them, **that they abstain from pollution of idols, and from fornication, and from things strangled, and from blood"*** (Acts 15: 20).

We have another "smoking gun" – the words *"...and from things strangled, and from blood."* This *certainly* refers to the 7th and last of the Seven Laws of the Sons of Noah, which forbids eating meat from an animal which was taken with cruelty.

Note also that the Apostle James is also referring to Noahide Laws 3 & 4, the laws which deal with idolatry and forbidden sexual relations. These were not mentioned in Genesis.

James then denies that the central Church ever instructed its missionaries that all Gentile converts had to undergo circumcision.

Then in Verse 29 James repeats what is required of Gentile converts to Christianity:

> *"...That ye abstain from meats offered to idols, and from blood, and from things strangled, and from fornication: from which, if ye keep yourselves, ye shall do well. Fare ye well."*

Paul *won* his first hearing before the Jerusalem Church.

But it didn't mean what most people think it means.

Most people believe that the Jerusalem Church began its existence as a church which practiced Jewish Law, but as time lapsed through the first decades of its existence, the Jerusalem Church gradually separated itself more and more from Judaism, and eventually became a totally new and different religion, largely following the ideas of the Apostle Paul.

Many people see this decision above as the first step in the process of separation of the two religions.

And at first glance it would seem so, since the Jerusalem Church certainly abrogated all need *for Gentiles* to undergo circumcision, which is of course a requirement for full conversion to Judaism.

But we now also know that the rest of Judaism never required its Noahide converts to undergo circumcision, either. And now that we know what the Seven Laws of the Sons of Noah are and can recognize them when we see them, we see that the Jerusalem Church did not at all abandon Judaism when it ruled that Gentile converts didn't need to undergo circumcision to become Christians. In fact, it is *precisely the opposite*!

This is the meaning of James' words: "*We are Jews!* We are Jews who follow the risen Jesus, *but we are still Jews!** And because we are Jews, we therefore keep and will keep the Commandments of Moses. Belief in the risen Jesus does not at all contradict, preclude, or nullify our observance of the Law.* And for this reason, and because the rest of Judaism allows Gentiles to convert to the Covenant of the Sons of Noah without circumcision, *we will therefore do the same, because we too are as Jewish as all other Jews, equally zealous to follow the Law of Moses, just like everybody else!*

When James made this decision, not only did the Church *not break away from* Judaism; *his decision affirmed the Church's desire to remain **within** Judaism and to maintain its observance of Mosaic Law* – for those Christians who were already fully Jewish.

The principle is simple: Full Jewish Law for followers of Jesus who were either born Jewish, or Gentiles who freely choose to undergo full conversion, and Noahide Law for those Gentiles who wish to follow Jesus without the burden of the entire Law.

About a half-dozen years lapsed between Paul's first and second trials. When he returned to Jerusalem, to face trial *before the Jerusalem Church* (and *not* the "bad Jews," *not* the Sadducees or the Pharisees or the Herodians or the Romans), we will see shortly that the Jerusalem Church still maintained its fidelity to Mosaic Law. It had not by so much as a single centimeter *ever* separated itself from Judaism.

* (There is no doubt that Christianity has always believed that Jesus died on a cross, and was resurrected from the dead. Many Christians believe that this belief immediately placed Christianity beyond the pale, caused the earliest of Christians (like St. Stephen) to be persecuted, placed Christianity outside of Judaism, that Jews ostracized Christians from the start, and that Christianity was a separate religion from its very conception.

(However, this view is impossible to sustain, because the Christian scriptures themselves make it plain, as we have seen above, that Christians were tolerated by the rest of the Jews, on the whole. If Christianity and Christians had been taboo to Jews, it is inconceivable that Rabbi Gamliel would have ruled so leniently as he did in Acts 5, and that the Jews would have tolerated their presence in the Great Temple.

(Many Christians – and Jews too for that matter – think it is impossible to believe both in a resurrected Jesus and nevertheless to continue to follow Mosaic Law.

(But this is arguably false. There is nothing in Judaism which prevents one from believing that a dead person can come back to life. Indeed, Judaism believes in *techiat ha-metim*, the resurrection of *all* the dead; we're *all* going to resurrect someday, according to Judaism. As far as Judaism is concerned, you can believe all you want that somebody never died, or rose from the dead – just as long as you don't believe that the resurrected person was God Himself.

(Elijah the Prophet himself raised a small boy from the dead, but nobody claims he or the boy were God. And likewise, in Acts 9, the Apostle Peter is said to have raised a woman named Tabitha (a.k.a. Dorcas) from the dead, but nobody says that Peter or Tabitha were God, either.

(Belief that someone has risen from the dead or never died in the first place is *not* intrinsically heretical in Judaism, and belief in that does *not*, in and of itself, excommunicate any Jew from the House of Israel. Judaism believes that at least seven once-living persons never died. To name three of them, Enoch never died (Genesis 5:24); Elijah the Prophet never died (see Chapter 4 above); and Sirach bat (daughter of) Asher (son of Jacob) never died.

(In other words, it *was* possible to believe in a resurrected Jesus and *still* be a practicing Jew in good standing. And Acts of the Apostles itself testifies to this.

(The only way that belief in a resurrected Jesus could get in the way of being accepted as a practicing Jew would be if such a Jew were to believe that the resurrected Jesus was God Himself.

(Judaism believes in miracles, and in the resurrection of the dead. Belief in resurrection simply means that one believes that God has the power to perform this miracle – and what God-fearing person would or could deny that? – and a Jew *could* believe that God had brought back Jesus to life and still be a Jew in good standing.

(All Judaism asks is that one does not infer from the resurrection of Jesus, that Jesus raised himself because he was himself divine.

(Judaism would say, one ought not confuse a miracle from

God with divinity itself.)

13) PAUL HAD LONG ABANDONED HIS BELIEF IN MOSAIC LAW

Most Christians understand that Paul abandoned his faith in Jewish Law, because he believed that only faith in Jesus Christ, and not obedience to the Law, could save one's soul – and, therefore, the Law of Moses has been set aside and nullified forever. This is already very well known – indeed, most Christians are *proud* of the Apostle Paul for teaching this, and think it is to Paul's credit that he did so. I therefore need no more than to cite a few examples from Paul's writing to illustrate the point, which I shall take from his Letter to the Galatians and the Romans.

THE EPISTLE TO THE GALATIANS

Chapter 2: 16:

> *"Knowing that a man is not justified* (saved) *by the works of the* (Mosaic) *law, but by the faith of Jesus Christ, even we have believed in Jesus Christ, that we might be justified by the faith of Jesus Christ, and not by the works*

of the law: for by the works of the law
shall no man be justified (that is to say,
will go to Heaven).*"*

No man is saved by Mosaic Law – neither Jew
nor Gentile.

Chapter 3: 10:

> *"For as many as are of the works of*
> *the law are under the curse: for it is*
> *written* (Deuteronomy 27: 26),
> *'Cursed is every one that continueth*
> *not in all things which are written in*
> *the book of the law to do them'."*

Not only can the Law not save anybody, but
following the Law *can only bring a curse on oneself!*
(Which makes one wonder – why did God waste His
time, giving a Law which can only bring a curse? In
the following verses, Paul actually tries to answer that
question.)

Chapter 3: 23 – 25:

> *"But before faith* (Jesus) *came, we*
> *were kept under the law, shut up into*

the faith which should afterwards be revealed.

Wherefore the law was our schoolmaster to bring us unto Christ, that we might be justified by faith.

But after that faith is come, we are no longer under a schoolmaster."

The Law was valid until Jesus came, but after he came, the Law is no longer valid.

Chapter 3: 28:

"There is neither Jew nor Greek, there is neither bond nor free, there is neither male nor female: for ye are one in Christ Jesus."

Jews no longer even exist! Because now we are all one under Jesus.

THE EPISTLE TO THE ROMANS

Chapter 2: 25:

"For circumcision verily profiteth, if thou keep the law, but if thou be a breaker of the law, thy circumcision is made uncircumcision."

A Jew(ish man) becomes a member of the Covenant of Abraham through circumcision. In fact, in the Yiddish language (which generally is a dialect of German), the very word for "circumcision" is *bris* – which means *"Covenant"* in Hebrew. Paul told the Galatians that all Jews break the Law. So in other words, if breaking the Law turns circumcision into non-circumcision, that means there can be no Jews, since all Jews break the Law, and in the process cease to be Jews. And indeed, Paul told the Galatians precisely that – there no longer was such a thing as a "Jew." And in that case, it cannot therefore even be the case that the Law was valid, as a "schoolmaster," until Jesus came. In Paul's logic, *the Law was **never** valid*.

Chapter 3: 1:

"What advantage then hath the Jew? Or what profit is there of circumcision?"

Chapter 3: 28:

"Therefore we conclude that a man is justified by faith without the deeds of the law."

14) THE SECOND TRIAL OF THE APOSTLE PAUL

It is now several years later. Jack Finegan (ibid) estimates that it is now late in the spring of the year AD 55 (CE).

The Jerusalem Church itself has now called Paul to return to Jerusalem, to answer certain accusations it has received which state that Paul has been a very, very naughty missionary, because he has taught, not only to his Gentile converts (which the central Nazarene Church in Jerusalem had given permission to do), but also to his *Jewish* converts (which he did *not* have permission to do), that they now not only may, but *should*, abandon their loyalty to Mosaic Law.

Of course we all know that Paul had done exactly that.

We pick up the story in Acts 20. Paul has traveled from Ephesus to Macedonia (Verse 1). He wants to sail to Syria, but instead goes east via Philippi (2 – 6). He visits several islands in the Aegean Sea, but bypasses Ephesus because he wants to return to Jerusalem before Pentecost (14 – 16).

In Chapter 21, Paul passes through other islands on his way to the Holy Land (21: 1 & 2) and eventually disembarks at Tyre in Lebanon (3).

In Verse 4, Paul spends seven days there, and is advised not to continue to Jerusalem.

In Verses 5 – 8, Paul sails to Caesarea.

Verses 10 & 11 then tell us:

"And as we tarried there many days, there came down from Jerusalem a certain prophet, named Agabus.

*And when he was come unto us, he took Paul's girdle, and bound his own hands and feet, and said, 'Thus saith the Holy Ghost, "So shall **the Jews** at Jerusalem bind the man that owneth this girdle, and shall deliver him into the hands of the Gentiles."'"*

QUESTION: **WHO** ARE THESE "**JEWS**"?

Luke doesn't tell us. But if these "Jews" are trying to capture Paul in order to turn him over to the Gentiles, a casual reader would naturally suppose that these must be the "bad Jews," and therefore must be some combination of Sadducees / Pharisees / Herodians, since these are the "bad Jews" which the Gospels mention and accuse many times.

But we will shortly see that *these "bad Jews" don't even know that Paul's in Jerusalem!* They don't learn of Paul's presence *until after Paul's trial before the Jerusalem Church has concluded,* when **the Romans** noted that a riot had broken out in Jerusalem *which was caused by* **Jewish Christians** *who'd accused Paul of preaching to* **Jewish Christians** *that they should abandon the Law.* And only after the Romans took Paul into protective custody did they refer the matter to the Sanhedrin.

First and foremost, one should *really* ask oneself, if Paul were in Macedonia when he received his summons to return to Jerusalem, then why on earth should Paul have respected or honored the summons? The Pharisees and the Sadducees and the Herodians had no authority outside Jerusalem, and therefore he could safely ignore *their* summons.

No – there was one, and *only* one source of authority in Jerusalem, which Paul would, and *could*, ever respect.

That was the authority of the Jerusalem Church itself.

Any authority which he himself possessed, came to him *solely* because the Jerusalem Church gave it to him, *and could revoke it anytime it pleased them.*

Evidently, the Jerusalem Church itself never recognized any "higher authority" which Paul claimed to have received directly from Jesus himself via a vision. There is absolutely nothing in *Acts of the Apostles* which even *hints* that the Jerusalem Church had ever even *heard* of Paul's vision. (Though, admittedly, one *might* reasonably suppose that Paul had to have informed the Jerusalem Church about his astounding switch from being the persecutor Saul to the Apostle Paul. The Jerusalem Church certainly would have wanted an explanation for his stunning reversal, and the story of his Vision certainly would have filled that bill.)

What a strange situation for Paul. On the one hand, he *knows* his authority *exceeds* that of the Jerusalem Church, because *he* received it *directly from Jesus* via his Vision, whereas those peasants who ran the Jerusalem Church only received *their* authority from the lesser, earthbound, corporeal Jesus, and for this reason *he* now *knows* that Mosaic Law is now null and void, even if *they* don't.

Which was Paul's problem; the Jerusalem Church itself *doesn't know this*. Never having received *any* instruction to the contrary from Jesus (see Matthew

5:17-18), neither from the earthly nor heavenly Jesus, they blithely continued to obey that Law which Paul *knows* is now null and void.

If Jesus had meant to nullify the Law, why did he tell only Paul, and not also the Jerusalem Church? We *know* that Peter also could receive visions. It would have made Paul's job *much* easier – and Jesus' job too, for that matter – if Jesus'd had the courtesy to let the rest of the Church know what he'd (supposedly) told Paul via his Vision.

Still, it was the Jerusalem Church and not Paul who possessed the authority of Jesus. (Whether or not Paul *actually* received any "higher authority" directly from Jesus is irrelevant, since it was *clearly* the authority of the Jerusalem Church which the rank-+-file followers of Jesus respected, and which ruled over Paul, whether he had real visions or not.) Any authority which Paul's converts saw in him, they knew he possessed, not from his Vision, which nobody but Paul had experienced, but rather from the visible Jerusalem Church, whom everybody knew was led by men who had been personal associates of Jesus.

So because it was the Jerusalem Church and not

Pharisees or Sadducees (whom he could ignore) who'd summonsed Paul to Jerusalem, Paul *had* to answer *their* summons and go to Jerusalem.

And so therefore, when Luke referred only to generic "Jews" who summonsed Paul, he attempted to mislead and confuse his readers, since most students of this scripture aren't careful enough to read between all the lines, and would suppose that Luke "obviously" must have been referring to the "bad Jews," the Sadducees / Pharisees / Herodians. (And I'm sorry to put it that way, but it really is the only explanation which makes sense.)

As we will see, "the Jews" who summonsed Paul to Jerusalem were *not* "the bad Jews," the Pharisees and the Sadducees and the Herodians, who didn't even know he was in town, *but instead were none other than the Jewish Christians who ran the Jerusalem Church*, the ones who'd personally known Jesus and his teachings, and not in Visions either, but instead from the living, real, corporeal Jesus. Some of these "Jews" were even Jesus' own blood relatives, such as the Apostle James.

> *"And after those days we took up our carriages, and went up to Jerusalem"*

(Verse 15).

"And when we were come to Jerusalem, the brethren received us gladly.

And the day following Paul went in with us unto James; and all the elders were present.

And when he (Paul) *had saluted them, he declared particularly what things God had wrought among the Gentiles by his* (Paul's) *ministry"* (Verses 17 – 19).

There is something curious here. Paul here speaks much about his ministry *among the Gentiles – but not a word about his ministry **unto the Jews***. But we *know* that Paul spent much of his time in *synagogues*.

But James cannot be put off this easily, for he has a *certain* question to ask of Paul...

"And when they heard it, they glorified the Lord, and said unto him (Paul), *'Thou seest, brother, how many*

*thousands of Jews there are which believe, **and they are all zealous of the law**'"* (Verse 20).

(Jewish Christians, who believed in Jesus *and* who followed the Mosaic Law. And whom the other Jews *tolerated* in this!)

And this is James' reason:

"As touching the Gentiles which believe, we have written and concluded (at Paul's first trial in AD 49; see Acts 15) **that they observe no such thing (Mosaic Law), SAVE ONLY THAT THEY KEEP THEMSELVES FROM THINGS OFFERED TO IDOLS, AND FROM BLOOD AND FROM STRANGLED, AND FROM FORNICATION"** (Verse 25).

Well, well, well. Once again we see our "smoking gun." The Jerusalem Church still supports the Seven Laws of the Sons of Noah. *And that therefore means, it also supports Judaism.* Here, the Jerusalem Church, in AD 55, is merely repeating what it told Paul in AD 49 – full Mosaic Law for Jewish Christians, Noahide Law for Gentile Christians. Nothing at all has changed. The Jerusalem Church *is still a Jewish church, still supporting Mosaic Law – unlike Paul.*

> *"'And they are informed of thee, **that thou teachest ALL THE JEWS which are among the Gentiles TO FORSAKE MOSES, saying that they ought not circumcise their children, neither to walk after the customs.'"***
>
> *What is it therefore? The multitude must needs come together: for they will hear that thou art come"* (Verses 21 & 22).

Uh-oh. Now Paul has a BIG problem…

For that's the case against Paul. Paul was *not ever* given any teaching authority from the Jerusalem Church to instruct the *Jewish* followers of Jesus they could now ignore the Law; Verse 21 above *proves* that.

But evidently the Jerusalem Church wasn't

certain, for they proposed to put the matter to a certain test…

> *"Do therefore this that we say to thee:*
> *We have four men which have a vow*
> *on them.*
>
> *Them take, and purify thyself with*
> *them, and be at charges with them,*
> *that they may shave their heads: and*
> *all may know that those things,*
> *whereof they were informed*
> *concerning thee, are nothing, **but that***
> ***thou thyself also walkest orderly, and***
> ***keepest the law"*** (Verses 23 & 24).

The Apostle James wants to know – does Paul observe Mosaic Law anymore, or doesn't he? That is the question which the Jerusalem Church put to him.

In the hindsight of history, it is clear to *us* that Paul had lost all belief in the Law, and no longer observed it.

I neither attack nor defend Paul. I merely *observe* this as the *truth*.

Paul now has a simple choice to make. He can either accept the test or refuse it.

Paul can tell the truth, or he can lie by trying to bluff his way through the test.

Why not tell the truth?

Does Paul not have a "higher authority" than the Jerusalem Church, one which he received directly from Jesus in a Vision? Really, if Paul *is* receiving Visions directly from Jesus, it *must* mean that his own authority outranks the authority of the Jerusalem Church. So, if this is the case, ought not Paul simply say so? Moreover, ought he not be *proud* to speak with an even higher authority than that of the Jerusalem Church? And finally, and simply as an honorable man, who should live with honor, ought not Paul simply tell the Jerusalem Church the truth – that he in fact *has* taught *Jews* to abandon the Law?

But instead of simply admitting this, whereby Paul could void any need to prove himself via a purification test, Paul instead chooses to take the purification test.

Why is taking the purification test a lie?

Because, it is an attempt to deceive the Jerusalem Church, for if Paul had simply admitted the truth, there'd have been no need to take the test. But if Paul successfully passes the test, the Jerusalem Church will think that he still believes in the Law, which we know he did not. Taking the purification test is Paul's bluff.

There is a saying in English: "When in Rome, do as the Romans do."

So what did Paul decide to do? Admit the truth, or attempt to deceive the Jerusalem Church with a bogus purification test?

Paul himself gives us a hint in his First Epistle to the Corinthians, *1 Corinthians 9:19–22*:

> *"For though I be free from all men, yet have I made myself servant unto all, that I might gain the more.*
>
> ***And unto the Jews I became as a Jew, that I might gain the Jews;*** *to them that are under the law, as under the law, that I might gain them that are*

under the law.

To them that are without law, as without law (being not without law to God, but under the law to Christ), that I might gain them that are without law.

To the weak became I as weak, that I might gain the weak: **I am made all things to all men**, *that I might gain them that are without law."*

"When in Rome, do as the Romans do." And, "When in Jerusalem, do as the Jews do."

Be all things to all men.

And that is what Paul did. He was in Jerusalem, so he did as the Jews do, and became a Jew, just as he admits in his Epistle to the Corinthians.

In order to continue to win souls for Christ, Paul has to be *free* to win souls. And to do that, he *must* have the support and back of the Jerusalem Church; he *must* have their authority. And that means, *he has to conceal the truth. He has to win this trial. He cannot admit that he's been teaching Jews to abandon the Law.*

And so Paul did as follows:

> *"Then Paul took the men, and the next day purifying himself with them entered into the temple, to signify the accomplishment of the days of purification, until that an offering should be offered for every one of them.*
>
> *And when the seven days were almost ended..."* (Verses 26 & 27).

He took part in a purification under a Mosaic Law that he himself absolutely no longer believed in – which, right there, means he was a *hypocrite* – in order to deceive the Christian Jews of the Jerusalem Church and make them believe that he still followed the Law, when he did not.

In plain English, *Paul lied.* (And I'm sorry if good Christians reading this are offended at these words – but what else can I say? Paul is found guilty and condemned, not by me, but rather *by the Christian canonized scripture!*)

And it almost worked. Paul went through this purification procedure, which he didn't believe in, for seven days. But then…

> *"And when the seven days were almost ended, the Jews which were of Asia* (today's Turkey), *when they saw him in the temple, stirred up all the people, and laid hands on him.*
>
> *Crying out, 'Men of Israel, help: This is the man, that teacheth all men every where against the people,* **and the law**, *and this place: and further brought Greeks also into the temple, and hath polluted this holy place.'*
>
> *(For they had seen before with him in the city Trophimus an Ephesian, whom they supposed that Paul had brought into the temple.)*
>
> *And all the city was moved, and the people ran together: and they took Paul, and drew him out of the temple: and forthwith the doors were shut"*

(Verses 27 – 30).

Who were the Jews who recognized Paul? Were they Christian Jews? Luke doesn't say. Perhaps it doesn't even matter because, whether or not they were Jewish Christians or just plain Jews, either way they obviously still followed the Law of Moses.

Luke gives us *no* evidence that the other parties of the Jews – the Herodians, the Pharisees, the Sadducees – were even aware that Paul was in Jerusalem. *This riot against Paul was clearly caused by Jewish Christians*, possibly together with non-believing ordinary Jews from the city.

> *"And as they were about to kill him, tidings came unto the chief captain of the band* (the "Italian band" of course – in other words, Romans; see *Acts 10*), *that all Jerusalem was in an uproar.*
>
> *Who immediately took soldiers and centurions, and ran down unto them: and when they saw the chief captain and the soldiers, they left beating of Paul"* (Verses 31 & 32).

* * *

With this, I come to the end of my presentation, for there is no further mention of the Seven Laws of the Sons of Noah anywhere in *Acts of the Apostles*, and I am unaware of any other mention of them in the entire New Testament.

The Romans obviously were totally unaware of Paul's presence in Jerusalem until the riot broke out.

The Romans actually didn't arrest Paul; rather, they placed Paul in protective custody until they could decide what to do with him.

Chapter 22 consists of Paul's long speech to the crowds in Jerusalem. It concludes with the Roman decision to scourge him – until Paul "pulls the ace out of his sleeve" and shows the Roman commander that he is a Roman citizen and therefore is inviolate.

Only then the Roman commander decides to summon the leaders of the Jews, definitely including the High Priest and the Sadducees, for another hearing. This is of course the first time *these* Jews have participated in *any* of the events already described.

The rest of the story is well-known, and I can stop here.

*　*　*

Paul clearly was a hypocrite (for submitting to a test under a Law that he no longer believed in) and a liar. He was also *possibly* a thief, because the normal way for a non-citizen to become a Roman citizen was to bribe a Roman magistrate with a lot of money, which Paul could have embezzled from the communities where he preached, who might have entrusted him with funds they intended for the maintenance of the Jerusalem Church. According to Acts 22:28, the Roman commander himself admits he obtained *his* Roman citizenship by buying it from some corrupt Roman magistrate.

This was so common and well-known in the 1st Century, the century to whom Luke wrote his words, that it seems that Luke tries to anticipate any reader's objection, and imply (or, in Luther's translation, nakedly says) that Paul was a Roman citizen from birth and therefore needed neither to embezzle nor bribe.

In 22:28, when the Roman commander tells Paul that he purchased his own citizenship, Luke quotes Paul to say, "But I was free-born." This is of course totally irrelevant, since millions of inhabitants of the Roman Empire were free-born but not ever citizens. And Martin Luther's translation makes it clear anyway that Paul is not merely claiming to be a free-born non-citizen, but is claiming that he was born into Roman citizenship too.

That is not impossible, but is very unlikely. Paul was a member of the Jewish minority which lived in Tarsus, a very remote city; how many Jews in such a backwater ever became Roman citizens?

When Luke repeats Paul's words, "But I was free-born," he brings to mind Shakespeare's famous line from *Hamlet*, "The lady doth protest too much, methinks," which means, when a guilty person vigorously denies an accusation, his very vigor is a sign he's guilty, because he's "protesting too much." And likewise here.

But is this even important?

Paul certainly *committed* sins – but *was* he a

sinner?

When one commits a sin, if the purpose is high and noble enough, has one really committed a sin?

And if you're the Apostle Paul, what purpose can be higher than winning souls for Jesus? Especially since Jesus himself spoke to Paul in Visions?

In *1 Corinthians 9*, Paul claimed a right to become all things to all men, in order to win souls for Christ.

And let's again look at what Paul said about circumcision in *Romans:*

Chapter 2: 25:

> *"For circumcision verily profiteth, if thou keep the law, but if thou be a breaker of the law, thy circumcision is made uncircumcision."*

Circumcision is a Commandment of God and is therefore a good thing, but according to Paul, personal sin can nullify this good thing and turn it into a bad thing.

Perhaps the opposite is also true? Can it be that a good purpose can transform a sin into a good thing? In other words, "The ends justify the means"?

I would wager that Paul thought so, and therefore he didn't believe he'd committed any sin – no sin of lying, or of embezzlement, or of anything else.

Paul had raised money from various Christian congregations to support the Mother Church in Jerusalem. I might presume that he'd embezzled some of this money to buy his Roman citizenship. But even if this is true, Paul might very well have rationalized to himself that he was committing no sin of theft, because he was spending the money for a higher purpose, for a Roman citizenship which could be his "Get out of Jail Free" card in the event he ever needed to pull this particular rabbit out of his hat. Because, Paul knew *the Truth* and those philistines in the Jerusalem Church, who didn't know the visionary, Heavenly Jesus as Paul did, did *not* know this Truth, and for this reason Paul needed to insure that he could continue to move about freely, to be able to preach this higher, superior Jesus to everybody.

I argue: Paul's belief in the Heavenly Jesus of his

Vision, in his mind justified using money intended to support Jesus' church for himself, in order to enable him better to preach the Truth about the *real Heavenly Jesus*. Thus, by embezzling the money (which I assume Paul did, despite Luke's words to the contrary), Paul was really doing a *good* thing, and thereby the "uncircumcision" of his sin was transformed into a circumcised virtue and good deed. So to speak, his sin of theft was turned into "untheft."

I don't need to decide or judge this. I leave it to the reader to decide for himself.

*   *   *

In this book, I set out to prove that one cannot properly understand certain portions of the New Testament, unless and until one has a knowledge of the Seven Laws of the Sons of Noah.

I believe I have now proven that. But that is a final judgment which I leave to the reader.

Two epilogues now follow.

15) EPILOGUE 1, THE DESPOSYNI

It is now the Year AD 318 (CE). It is almost 300 years since Jesus walked on the earth. A lot has happened in the meanwhile. The Jews have fought and lost two horrible wars with the Romans, and have been exiled from the Holy Land and scattered all over the Roman Empire. Jews have been banned from Jerusalem.

But Christianity has actually become the official religion of the Roman Empire!

The Emperor Constantine had fought and won the Battle of the Milvian Bridge several years earlier, in the name of Jesus Christ, and has legalized Christianity, this in AD 312. The all-important Nicean Council hasn't yet taken place, but that is only seven years in the future.

And Pope Sylvester is the Bishop of Rome, the Successor of Peter the first Pope. Sylvester is the first pope who ever died peacefully in bed, since most if not all of his predecessors underwent cruel martyrdom. He is officially a Catholic saint to this day, and his feast-day is December 31, which is why to this day all of Europe has named New Year's celebrations "Sylvester."

And on a certain day in 318, he is meeting eight very strange men, who have traveled all the way from Jerusalem to see him.

These are the *desposyni. They are blood relatives of Jesus who **still** run the original Jerusalem Church*, just as James led the Jerusalem Church in the last years of the Great Temple. Amazingly enough, a remnant of them actually survived the two wasteful wars the Romans waged against Judea, which resulted in the expulsion of practically all Jews from the Holy Land.

Only *desposyni* may lead the Jerusalem Church. And only relatives of Mary count; relatives of Joseph do *not* count. Which tells us, the *desposyni* must have believed in the Virgin Birth, which is no Jewish belief.

But they are still Jews, and descendants of those Jewish blood relatives of Jesus who ran the Church in the days of Paul, who believed *in Judaism*, and who ran a *Jewish* church which *might fairly* be described as *the Jerusalem Synagogue of Jesus Christ*.

It's a miracle that this Church still even exists – but it does.

They had even appointed their own bishops to run churches in places like Antioch, which were satellite churches of the Jerusalem Mother Church. But Pope Sylvester has replaced these leaders with men of his own, and so the *desposyni* have come to Rome to ask Pope Sylvester to reconsider and let them appoint their own bishops.

And Pope Sylvester *refused* their request!

Why would he do that? Wasn't it a nice thing to have a church in Jerusalem which was actually led by Jesus' and Mary's own blood relatives?

But probably Pope Sylvester couldn't trust them, fearing that they might be too Jewish and not sufficiently Pauline, so he replaced them with his own men. And so the last remnant of the original Church of Jesus and his brother(?)/cousin(?) James vanished into history.

16) EPILOGUE 2: WHAT COULD HAVE BEEN?...

We have seen that there was a competition in the early Church between the Jewish ideas of the Jerusalem Church and the new and non-Jewish ideas of the Apostle Paul.

It took the Jerusalem Church almost 20 years to realize that Paul was preaching abrogation of the Law, not only to Gentile converts, which he was permitted to do, but also to *Jewish* converts, which he was *not* permitted to do.

But the Jerusalem Church (Synagogue of Jesus?) finally caught onto Paul and proved he was preaching what they regarded as *heresy*, and this ended, or almost entirely ended Paul's entire missionary career, since *Acts of the Apostles* informs us that Paul was held in jail for several years, and then traveled to Rome while under arrest, experienced shipwreck at Malta en route, and eventually made it to Rome, where he was held under house arrest for at least two years, and is said to have been martyred during the persecutions of the Christian movement by the Emperor Nero.

We have seen that the original Jerusalem Church was *never* allied with Paul, but instead was allied with the rest of *Judaism*.

Acts of the Apostles has given us valuable evidence that the knowledge and practice of the Seven Laws of the Sons of Noah were very widely known in the last years of the Temple.

So we arrive at my question: *What would have happened if the Jews had not revolted against Rome about eleven years later?*

The Jerusalem Church had a better reputation and more prestige than Paul ever had. We know that even Paul respected the Jerusalem Church's ultimate authority; else, when the Church summonsed him from Macedonia to Jerusalem, why would he have made a very long and difficult journey to answer their summons, when he had to have known they'd already caught onto the truth and knew he'd been preaching a forbidden doctrine to Jewish Christians?

If Paul knew he were guilty as charged, really, he should have just stayed in Macedonia and broken with the main Church immediately. Many other heretics have done so in the past. In the eyes of the Catholic Church, Martin Luther himself was such a "heretic" when, in his own eyes, he was in the right, and the Catholic Church was wrong.

What *is* a "heretic"? Merely somebody who thinks he knows certain doctrines better than the official church from whence he comes. And what makes a *church* "official"? And when a church is "official," does that mean that *everything* it says is correct and Orthodox, as a matter of definition?

Is any official church always correct because it has power? Or is any official church powerful because it is correct, *Deo gratiae*?

In 1870, the Catholic Church promulgated a doctrine that when the Pope speaks *ex cathedra*, he speaks *infallibly* – I suppose, because all the popes claim they, *and nobody else*, possess "the Keys to the Kingdom." They claim Apostolic Succession, which means, all the popes – the Bishops of Rome – who followed Peter, possess the "Keys to the Kingdom" because, as we've seen (Matthew 16), Jesus gave these Keys to Peter, who (in the Catholic tradition) became the first Pope – the first Bishop of Rome – and passed along these Keys to Linus his successor, and so forth, all the way to the present Pope Benedict XVI (or whoever will become his successor; I write these words shortly after Pope Benedict's startling resignation).

Yes, Jesus gave the "Keys to the Kingdom" to Peter, but after him, who or what was the "Church"? When Martin Luther rebelled against the Catholic Church, he believed that *he* represented the *True* Church.

If Paul truly received his Visions from the *heavenly* Jesus, did these not count for more than the visible authority which the *earthly* Jesus gave to the Jerusalem Church? If Paul truly believed that, then, when the Jerusalem Church summonsed him to come to Jerusalem to answer their questions, he should have broken with the Jerusalem Church *immediately*.

Perhaps – but that's not what he did. Instead, he surrendered himself to the authorities of the Jerusalem Church.

Why? Surely he didn't respect or believe that their authority was higher than his. Did he surrender because he though it was useless to resist the authority of the Jerusalem Church, notwithstanding the superiority of his Visions? Probably, in the end, he did so because even he could see that his flock placed the authority of the Jerusalem Church over his own.

As far as we know, never again did Paul ever preach, as a free man, before any large crowd. To put it simply, *Paul lost his second trial*, and this crippled his missionary activities permanently.

We know the following: a) The Jerusalem Church was against Paul. b) Paul accepted and respected the higher authority of the Jerusalem Church. c) Converting to Judaism, in the second class, as a Noahide convert, was very popular in the Roman Empire. d) The Jerusalem Church decided to accept such converts because all of Judaism did. e) *And the Jerusalem Church never left Judaism.*

The reason Paul's gentilized version of Christianity prevailed, and not the avowedly Jewish version of the original Jerusalem Church – the reason Christianity became what we know and see today – was because, shortly after Paul's second trial, the Jerusalem Church was wrecked by the Roman – Jewish War of AD 66 – 73.

But what if there had been no war, and Judaism had been allowed to spread peacefully throughout the Roman Empire?

Would Judaism (including of course Noahide Judaism) have become the Official State Religion of the Roman Empire in the future, and not Christianity? Could Judaism and not Christianity have become the world's dominant religion?

If so, what might have become of the Pauline version of Christianity, which today is the universal general form of Christianity? In the 3rd Century, a number of major Christian heresies arose, such as Marcionism, which were a big deal in their time, but which today few have ever even heard of. If there had been no war and the original Jerusalem Church of the Apostles had remained intact after 70 AD, would it eventually have consigned today's Pauline Christianity to the same anonymous ash-heap of history to which Marcionism has been consigned?

If the Jerusalem Church had successfully suppressed Paul's Christian movement permanently, would a Jewish-Christian Church have ultimately triumphed, one of course along the lines established by the Jerusalem Church before the destruction of

Jerusalem in AD 70, so that a different form of Christianity, Jewish and not Pauline, would exist today?

Would Christianity in *any* form at all exist today; would a Jewish Christianity have become one of a number of forms of Judaism, all living together peacefully? In our own world, we see today that in the world of Orthodox Judaism, there are sects of Chassidic Jews who regard their grand rabbis as holy prophets, and they live together peacefully alongside non-Chassidic Orthodox Jews, who don't share such beliefs. Perhaps this could have become the fate of Jesus in our world – a man followed by some believing and practicing Jews, not by others?

Would Noahide Jewish Christianity have become the Official State Religion of the Roman Empire?

But as it was, time was almost up for Jerusalem. Soon thereafter they had a disastrous war with Rome. It almost destroyed the Jerusalem Church, and certainly annihilated its ability to compete with, and speak against, Pauline Christianity. Pauline Christianity became the standard for all of Christianity, because there was no more Jerusalem Church to stand against it. Pauline Christianity had the entire field unto itself, and the rest is history.

What could have been, had there been no Jewish War of AD 66 - 73?...We will never know...

Made in the USA
Las Vegas, NV
24 November 2022